At Least 1836 Things You Ought to Know about Texas but Probably Don't

Doris L. Miller

Drawings by Jennifer Remy Renfrow

Republic of Texas Press
an imprint of
Wordware Publishing, Inc.

Library of Congress Cataloging-in-Publication Data

Miller, Doris L.
    At least 1836 things you ought to know about Texas--but probably
    don't. Doris L. Miller
        p.   cm.
    Includes index.
    ISBN 1-55622-324-2
    1. Texas--Miscellanea.   I. Title.   II. Title: At least one
    thousand eight hundred thirty six things you ought to know about
    Texas--but probably don't.
    F386.5.M55   1993
    976.4--dc20   93-49541
                                            CIP

ISBN 1-55622-324-2
10 9 8 7 6 5 4 3 2
9408

All inquiries for volume purchases of this book should be addressed to
Wordware Publishing, Inc., at the above address. Telephone inquiries may
be made by calling:

(214) 423-0090

Contents

Photos by Doris Miller.

Line drawings by Jennifer Remy Renfrow from Miller's photos.

Introduction

About two years ago I went to a local bookstore to purchase a trivia book on Texas. Much to my dismay, there weren't any that really caught my eye. This is not to say that there weren't any trivia books—goodness, no! There were question and answer books with too many actors and football players and that sort of trivia. There were really good books on only one subject—bed and breakfasts, festivals, ghost stories, Indian legends and others. The *Texas Travel Handbook*, put out by the Texas Department of Highways and Public Transportation, provided the type of information I was craving, but I wanted more. At this point I decided to fill a niche.

Several letters to publishers later, it was decided that the idea might have a chance. So where do you go from here? You write to the local Chamber of Commerce of the town you are interested in—and this is what I did, hundreds of them! My poor mail lady! She started leaving my mail on the doorstep since the two feet of mail I was receiving daily didn't want to go in our standard mailbox! I am surprised she didn't knock on the door and ask me what I was doing! And my poor husband! When the piles started to accumulate he threw up his hands and ran.

After the information came in, I had to read all the wonderful information these people sent me. There were travel brochures, statistics on their town, there were handwritten letters and even area phone books. The people were so very kind, and believe me, I read each and every piece of information that was sent—well, I did skip the phone books. I even read the advertisements, where I found several good things for the book.

Out of the hundreds of requests I sent, there was only one sour puss in the whole lot (probably an implant to Texas!). This chamber leader offered me a history book of their town for $70.00 and then told me I couldn't use the information without their authorization!

Introduction

The other several hundred chambers, historical societies, and individuals were so very kind. They sent me more information than I could have possibly used—and I read it all! I hope they will forgive me for not using all the information. I did not leave out any one of them on purpose, but I did have to pick and choose material for the book. I hope they smile when they read the book and know that they are the reason the book was written. I have a special thank-you section in the back for these special people.

People who have seen my collection of information expect me to write another book. I probably won't have a chance to write a sequel—I will be too busy writing an update to correct and clarify this one! As I was writing I would find three towns claiming a certain title, two counties claiming to have the most whatever, and believe me, it is a little hard to distinguish who is the real holder of the title sometimes! So I know that I am going to get letters—lots and lots of letters. But who knows, that may be a wonderful book in itself!

So, please, as you read this bit of Texas truism, keep in mind that I did not put anything in it that I knew was untrue, but since almost all of the information did come from Texans trying to sell me on their town, you may not want to use it as a textbook. I hope you have fun with the book—I had a lot of fun putting it together for you.

A book is not complete without dedications, so here are mine:

To my husband, Terry, for his patience and tolerance.
To my daughter, Stephanie, who thought I was crazy
—but helped me anyway.

Chapter 1 ────────────────

Tall Tales and True Stories

Very old gravesite in the Mesquite Cemetary. Beautiful carved headstones tell the story of our pioneer ancestors.

Chapter 1

Crane County was organized in August 1927 and the first county officials were elected on September 3, 1927. A Bible could not be found, so the officials were sworn in with a Sears & Roebuck catalog!

* * * * *

The **Caldwell County Courthouse** was completed in 1894. The courthouse had electricity but no indoor plumbing. There is a story that when the broom closets at the courthouse were converted to restrooms, the county judge ordered them padlocked after he got the first water bill!

* * * * *

The last hanging in the **Gonzales jail** happened March 18, 1921. The story is told that Albert Howard, while he was in jail, kept telling everyone that he was innocent and if they hanged him anyway, the clock on the courthouse would prove his innocence by never keeping accurate time again. The clock never did keep time after Howard's hanging, so the clock works were changed, but to this day, none of the four faces keep the same time!

* * * * *

The story of the **Lady In Blue** is told about Mother Maria de Agreda in the 1620s. When she was born her mother had no birth pains and knew she was blessed by God. She became a nun at the age of twelve and soon started to experience visions. In one of her visions she was transported to America from Spain and commanded to preach to the Indians in the New Mexico area. Though she spoke only Spanish, the Indians in her vision understood every word she spoke. The Indians were shocked at her appearance and called her the "Lady In Blue" because of a bright blue cloak she wore. Over the next 10 years, Maria made over 500 vision trips to New Mexico and Texas. She provided her local priest with vivid details of the area she had visited and he believed the miracles. The missionaries of the area in question began getting reports from the Indians about a strange woman who came to them to teach. Father Benavides, who was at the Isleta Mission on the Rio Grande, was visited by a group of Jumanos Indians from central Texas requesting missionaries be sent to their village. The Indians explained that the Lady In Blue had converted them and told them to travel to New Mexico to request missionaries. He sent two missionaries to their village near where

2

San Angelo is today. When the men arrived they were greeted with the tribe carrying crosses and requesting baptism. Upon questioning the tribe, the missionaries found they had been well taught and knew their catechism. Several years later Father Benavides left New Mexico and returned to Spain. One of the first things he did was to visit Maria and question her about the area. She provided details about the Rio Grande and the surrounding area that only someone who had actually been there would know—and some things which the Father would not tell. She told him of the little crosses and the rosaries that she had given to the Indians and he remembered seeing these things when the Indians came to the mission. He was convinced that she had truly made the vision trips as she had claimed.

* * * * *

One of the tall tales of Texas is a story about **Texas Ranger Jack Hays**. Seems that Jack was sweet on Susan Calvert, whose father owned the Magnolia Hotel. One day Susan accepted an invitation from another young man to go down to the river. When they returned, Major Hays proceeded to catch and hang the young man. Texas tale or fact? Jack and Susan were married in 1847 at the Magnolia Hotel and, on their way from the ceremony, were met by 14 buggy loads of girls who had a picnic lunch waiting to help Jack celebrate!

* * * * *

There is a tale about the outlaw **Will Carver** in Sonora. Will Carver, a member of the Hole in the Wall Gang, and George Kilpatrick were shot by Sheriff Briant and his deputies while in a local feed store. The date was April 2, 1901. Mr. Kilpatrick was turned loose because he was not wanted for anything, but Will Carver was taken to the courthouse where he later died of his wounds. He was buried in an unmarked grave in the Sonora Burial Park. Soon after the burial, a marker, bearing only the date of his death, was placed on his grave. No one knows who put it there, but local people believed outlaw friends placed the marker on his grave during the night. There are others who believe that the man buried was a cowboy that was misidentified on purpose, and Carver went to Mexico to live. There are tales of men who swore that they drank with Carver in Acuna, Mexico, after that fateful day. Fact or fiction?

* * * * *

John Singer, whose brother was famous for the Singer Sewing Machine, and his wife, Johanna, became shipwrecked on Padre Island. They built their home of driftwood around 1847, and in 1861, before leaving the island in fear of the Civil War, they buried approximately $62,000 in coins and jewelry. When the war was over, the Singers returned to the island around 1865, only to discover their treasure was lost in the shifting sands. As far as anyone knows, the treasure is still buried in the sand now known as Money Hill.

* * * * *

Sweeny was the name of the first land holder and of the first postmaster of the town of Sweeny. No one is quite sure which the town was named after, the father or the son. Actually, it is quite by accident that John Sweeny owned the land at all. When he lived in Tennessee he sent his two sons to town to sell some mules, and instead of bringing home the money, they brought home a Texas land grant! Seems at the time there was a strong "move to Texas" atmosphere in town, and they got caught up in the excitement with their father's money! Needless to say, ol' Dad was not exactly pleased with the young lads. The papers were put aside and in 1831 John's brother and one son went to Texas to look at the land. It was two years later when John, his wife, nine children, and 250 slaves made the move to Texas.

* * * * *

The community of **Aransas Pass** was organized three times. The first two times didn't work out, but the third time in 1909 a firm called Burton and Danforth platted out the town and advertised lots for $100.00 each. Problem was that the town was "oversold" by $3 million dollars and they had to return the money. Since they were selling the lots by mail, the post office claimed that the way they were drawing for lots made it a lottery and the whole operation was illegal!

* * * * *

James Britton "Britt" Bailey was a pioneer Texan who came here in 1918 and died in 1933. He is buried in Angleton. At his request he was buried standing up, facing west, with his gun at his side. He did not want anyone looking down on him even after his death.

* * * * *

The hamburger got its beginning in the 1880s on the courthouse square in **Athens**. There was a small cafe on the square where Fletcher Davis (Uncle Fletch) served a sandwich of homemade bread, meat patty, hot mustard, onion, and a pickle on the side. The sandwiches were so popular that in 1904 a group of businessmen sent Uncle Fletch to the St. Louis World's Fair to sell his sandwiches, and the hamburger was introduced to the world. The first Uncle Fletch Davis Memorial World Hamburger Cook-Off was held in 1984, sponsored by the Chamber of Commerce, to commemorate the installation of a historical marker at the cafe site.

✳ ✳ ✳ ✳ ✳

Baird had only one legal hanging, in 1906. Seems Alberto Vargas stabbed Miss Emma Blakley because she did not return his affections, and he then attempted to kill himself by stabbing. The man was saved from death and then hanged.

✳ ✳ ✳ ✳ ✳

In 1983 the Boerne Independent School District gave the Boerne Area Historical Preservation Society an old German Bible. That old tattered Bible has now been identified as a rare, authentic, 1614 Luneburg Bible. There is believed to be only three of these Bibles remaining, and the one in **Boerne** is the only one of the three that has a coat of arms on the cover.

✳ ✳ ✳ ✳ ✳

The Treue der Union Monument, in **Comfort**, commemorates the Nueces River Massacre. On August 12, 1862, a group of Comfort area Unionists, on their way to Mexico to avoid the Confederate draft, were ambushed and 36 men were killed. After the Civil War ended, a group recovered the bones and brought them back to Comfort for burial. The monument, placed in 1866, is the only monument to the Union outside of National Cemeteries in Confederate territory.

✳ ✳ ✳ ✳ ✳

Borger's earliest jail was a log! The prisoners sat on the ground chained to the log!

✳ ✳ ✳ ✳ ✳

Ringgold is located at US Highway 81 and US Highway 287. In 1936, when the two roads were being constructed, the sand for the construction was taken from a nearby sand pit. When they noticed that the sand had a "sparkle" to it, they had it assayed and found that it did contain gold. The owner tried to mine the remaining gold, but it's estimated value only came to $250,000. There is estimated to be more than $30,000 in gold dust along 39 miles of road.

* * * * *

The **Justin Boot Company** began at a Spanish fort under a tree. There is one story that H.J. Justin came to town with only 25 cents and so he set up shop under a tree in town. The cowboys would order their boots as they drove the herd up the trail and would pick them up on the way back home.

* * * * *

Nancy Hill was a notorious horse thief in the 1860s and early 1870s. In December of 1873, she was caught in the act and hanged without a trial. Nancy Hill was the only woman ever hanged in Montague County and was probably the first white person hanged as well.

* * * * *

Forestburg only had one bank and it was closed after bandits robbed the bank and locked the bank employees and customers in the vault and left. The Forestburg Bank operated from 1917 to 1931.

* * * * *

Luler Wiggins died at the age of 15 in 1890 and is buried in the Perryman Cemetery outside of Forestburg. After she died her family went to New Mexico, but her father returned two years later with a headstone for her grave. Because the weather was so bad, the father left the headstone with a shopkeeper to put on the grave when the weather cleared, but the stone was forgotten. In 1927 a fire almost destroyed all of the businesses, and in the cleanup, most of the debris was carried to a creek and dumped. In 1957 a man digging sand from the creekbed discovered the stone, and it was finally placed on the grave, 65 years later.

* * * * *

The only town in Texas known to have been named by a president of the United States is **Burkburnett**. The town was named by President Theodore Roosevelt in honor of Samuel Burk Burnett who had invited Roosevelt to a wolf hunt on the Red River. Since there was already a Burnet, Texas, Burnett's middle and last names were combined to form the name of the new town in 1907.

* * * * *

A block of marble from the Samuel E. Holland holdings, three miles south of **Burnet,** was sent to Washington, D.C. as Texas' contribution to the Washington Monument.

* * * * *

There is a story in **Brady** about the prisoner of war internment camp east of town during World War II. Although three prisoners did escape in April 1944 and were captured nine days later headed for Mexico, there is another story about an escape tunnel. Supposedly, the prisoners dug a tunnel from their barracks floor out under the fence to a nearby field. The prisoners took the dirt out in their pockets and put it in the compound to keep the guards from finding fresh dirt piled around. It is not known whether any escaped via the tunnel, but the story tells of the prisoners using the tunnel to go to town to visit for a while and then returning to camp the same way!

* * * * *

In 1860 a toll bridge was built across the Trinity River about a mile and a half southwest of the present Bridgeport City Hall. The town began to grow right after the bridge was built and it is assumed that the town got its name from this first enterprise—thus, **Bridgeport.**

* * * * *

In 1891 the courthouse was complete in **Columbus** and the whole town celebrated—including the six prisoners who broke out of the jail while the party had everyone's attention elsewhere!

* * * * *

Herman Yezak, a first lieutenant during World War II, a Bremond native, and a Texas Aggie, was elected to the Texas Legislature in 1944. What makes his election so unusual is that during the whole campaign, Mr. Yezak was out of the country! He had postcards printed asking for votes and mailed the cards from Rome, Italy!

* * * * *

The last jailbreak in **Bremond** was somewhat different. A carpenter had worked on the jail, got his pay, and promptly spent it at a local saloon where he began to start fights across town. Of course he was arrested and taken to jail, but during the night, he loosened the hinges and removed the door and went home. The next morning, the carpenter was called back to the jail to replace the door—and put the hinges on the outside of the door!

* * * * *

Robber's Roost was located in the far northeast corner of Robertson County, east of Bremond. Famous and not-so-famous outlaws used the area for a hideout. The woods and the wilderness made a great hiding place when the law came around, and when the coast was clear, a bell would ring. That signal bell is now on the roof top of Howard Dunn's home on Highway 14, north of Bremond.

* * * * *

Calvert had one of the first power and ice plants in Texas and maybe the only beer drinking fire horse, named Dan. Dan was owned by the Calvert Ice, Water & Electric Co. The building was built in 1886, under contract with Adolph Busch to warehouse the beer for Mr. Busch. When the fire department would meet, they broke out the beer—including half a barrel for Dan. Dan never showed any ill effects and was always up at dawn delivering beer and ice from store to store, waiting until the delivery was un-loaded—without a driver! The Calvert Ice, Water & Electric Co. building was destroyed in April 1975 by a tornado, two weeks after it was named to the National Historic Register.

* * * * *

Myra Bell Shirley came to Calvert with her parents to start a livery stable and wagon yard. Legend says she went to Sterling several times to deliver secret documents from Confederate officers. Some say she was a Confederate spy, but then she started to run with the wrong crowd—Frank and Jesse James and the Younger Brothers. Myra was supposedly shot in the back by her Indian lover, Sam Starr, but a man in Bowie claimed his grandfather told him that Myra was hung on a tree on his land after being caught stealing a horse. Myra was better known as Belle Starr.

* * * * *

First Monday Trade Days, in **Canton**, dates back over a hundred years; records exist back to the mid-1800s. The first Monday of the month was set aside for county residents to settle lawsuits at the courthouse, and while they waited they could buy supplies and sell and trade animals. There is one tale of two men who came to First Monday, took a liking to one another's wife, obtained divorces and remarried, and went home with new wives—now that's tall tradin'! First Monday attracts over 100,000 people each month and has never been canceled due to the weather.

* * * * *

Did you know there is a Fox Hound Cemetery at Boles Field? Since 1941 a plot of federal land in the Boles Field Recreational Area, east of **Center**, has been used to lay to rest the faithful. The cemetery is not for every hound since the East Texas Fox Hunters Association must approve each dog laid to rest in the cemetery. In 1941 a dog by the name of Dawson Stride, Texas' first recognized field champion, died of overexertion in a chase at Boles Field. The dog's owner, Hinkle Schillings, and his friends received permission to bury the dog on government property by the U.S. Forest Service. It is possibly the only dog graveyard on federal land.

* * * * *

In April 1920, Lige Daniels, a young black man, was accused of killing a woman, Mrs. Hall, with a hoe. He was arrested and taken to jail, but a lynching party took him from the jail and hanged him from a large red oak tree on the courthouse square in **Center**, Shelby County. According to the story, the limb he was hanged from died and the rope turned black. Other hangings took place on the dead limb and part of the rope was still on the limb in 1936. In 1982 several of the limbs died, and eventually the whole tree died and was removed from the square.

* * * * *

Claude was named after the first railroad engineer to reach the town. The town had no name, so he requested they name the town after him. His name was Claude Ayers, and he is buried in the town cemetery.

* * * * *

Charles Lindbergh crashed into the side of a hardware store in Camp Wood in 1924. Lindbergh offered to pay for the damage, but the owner said the advertising value was worth more than the damage.

* * * * *

Rumors of buried treasure in the **Clear Lake** area have been around since before the Civil War. In the 1890s a Galveston newspaper often carried stories of farmers digging up gold coins as they worked the soil and cleared the trees. Gold coins have turned up very recently in Anahuac, across Galveston Bay.

* * * * *

The St. Louis Society Building, in **Castroville**, built in the 1850s, was a saloon for much of its days. There is a story of a one-eyed barkeeper that would take out his glass eye and leave it on the counter when he had to leave. He always instructed his glass eye to "watch things for me" when he left! They say he never lost a dime.

* * * * *

One night, during Prohibition, in **Castroville**, a poker game was going on with many of the players being local bootleggers. The group found out that a group of revenue officers had arrived, so someone was sent to fetch the hearse. The man responsible for the hearse hitched up his team of mules and parked outside the house. One man held the team while another stood with his hat over his heart. Not wanting to disturb a family in mourning, the revenue officers passed the house, and the poker game continued undisturbed. The old horse-drawn hearse has been preserved and is on display at the Institute of Texan Cultures in San Antonio.

* * * * *

On October 8, 1932, Raymond Hamilton, a member of the Bonnie and Clyde Barrow gang, robbed the First State Bank of **Cedar Hill**. After Hamilton read in the paper that the bank president hid a portion of the money, he went back and robbed it a second time.

* * * * *

Around 1928 the **Cedar Hill Bull Circle** was created to provide a community bull to service the many milk cows in town. A Jersey bull was brought from Michigan, and the Bull Circle was in charge of taking care of his needs and getting him from one farm to the next.

* * * * *

The **Buffalo Gap Cemetery**, the oldest in Taylor County, dates back to the mid-1800s where the first grave was believed to be for a fellow that cheated at cards.

* * * * *

Conrad Hilton began his career as "Innkeeper of the World" when he purchased his first hotel, the Mobley, in **Cisco**, in 1919. Hilton came to Cisco to purchase a bank, but the absentee owner raised the promised sale price and he backed off of the deal. Hilton was really disappointed when he couldn't rent a hotel room for the night—the hotel owner was renting all available rooms for 8-hour shifts! Hilton learned there was money to be made in things other than banks and oil and promptly made a deal to purchase the hotel from Mr. Mobley. He soon made plans to expand his hotel interest to other Texas cities, and the rest, as they say, is history!

* * * * *

There is one account that tells that **Delta County** was formed from a portion of Lamar and Hopkins counties between the forks of the Sulphur River. Dr. E.P. Becton, a Sulphur Springs resident and legislator, proposed the new county because people from the region couldn't get to their county seats in Tarrent or Paris in bad weather because of the condition of the river forks, and therefore they needed their own seat of government closer to the people. The real reason, it is told, is that by sectioning off this area of land, the new geographical center of Hopkins County became Sulphur Springs, which wanted to become the county seat. By organizing Delta County, the way was cleared for Sulphur Springs to become the county seat of Hopkins County.

* * * * *

After 37 years, **Lick Skillet** became **Crosby**. The story goes that East Texas oxen team drivers would stop at the spring to drink and fix supper—licking their skillets clean—so the "Lick Skillet" name stuck. The area was a good one to make camp after a long day's ride because of the spring and the abundant game.

* * * * *

The **Masonic Hall of Crosby**, Sampson Lodge #231, was organized in 1859, moved to Lynchburg when the town became the trading center, and moved back to Crosby after the 1900 hurricane. That storm destroyed the Masonic Hall in Lynchburg—but the jewels of the lodge were found in the bay after the storm. They had been tied to a door knob and the door was what was found floating! The jewels were taken to Crosby when the lodge was rebuilt, and on the 100th anniversary of the lodge, in 1959, they were given to the Grand Masonic Lodge Museum.

* * * * *

Laughlin Air Force Base, in the Del Rio area, was used as a training base for the 408th Strategic Reconnaissance Wing, a highly secret U-2 unit. In October of 1962, this unit was credited with the first pictures of the Soviet missile build-up in Cuba. The only

11

casualty of the crisis was Laughlin's Major Rudolf Anderson whose U-2 was shot down over Cuba.

* * * * *

Judge Roy Bean once held a world championship prize fight between Australia's Bob Fitzsimmons and Ireland's Peter Mahar. Both the U.S. and Mexico had rulings prohibiting the fight, so Judge Bean held it on a sandbar in the middle of the Rio Grande. The fight was in February of 1896, and Fitzsimmons won by a knockout in one minute and 35 seconds.

* * * * *

Legend calls **Judge Roy Bean** a hanging judge, but there is no record that he ever sentenced a man to be hanged. Judge Bean did run a horse thief out of town, after taking his money and his gun, and threatening him with a noose if he ever came to town again.

* * * * *

The city of **Elgin** owes its existence to a major flood of the Colorado River in 1869. The railroad had just surveyed an area 10 miles east of what is Elgin today, called McDade, to install a line southwest to the Colorado River between Bastrop and Webberville. The Colorado River went 60 feet over its banks and flooded a large area on which the railroad had planned to build. Needless to say, the railroad moved, and a one-square-mile area was deeded for the new town of Elgin.

* * * * *

In the early days of **Fort Worth** there was an area of saloons and dance halls that was called **Hell's Half Acre**. One such establishment advertised "service in the saddle." Hell's Half Acre was a favorite "rest stop" for the Hole in the Wall Gang, Butch Cassidy, and the Sundance Kid, between jobs.

* * * * *

The first automobile accident in the state of Texas happened in **Forney** on October 5, 1899. Col. E.H.R. Green purchased an automobile from a St. Louis company, and George P. Dorris, the designer and chief engineer of the company, came to Terrell to give Col. Green driving instructions. On their way from Terrell to Dallas, the car was crowded off the road, by a farm wagon, into a gully, thus creating the first Texas automobile accident. The repairs took about an hour by a Forney blacksmith, then the two men continued on their way. The trip from Terrell to Dallas took five hours and 20 minutes, and when they got to Ross Ave. in Dallas, the car knocked down a telephone pole—guess this is the second Texas accident!

* * * * *

There is a legend of an Indian girl named Emily that took place long ago in West Texas near **Fort Davis**. After a battle with the Apache Indians, a young Indian girl was taken to the fort hospital where they named her Emily. She fell in love with a young soldier as she was recovering from her wounds, but when the young man did not return her feelings, Emily went back to her tribe. Months after she left the fort, she overheard the leaders' plan to attack and burn the fort. She returned to warn the young soldier, but she was shot by a sentry who thought she was an enemy. Emily lived long enough to warn the fort of the coming attack. Emily was buried with a wooden marker which simply says "Indian Squaw—Killed by Accident." The state of Texas erected a monument to Indian Emily in 1936, made of granite, with an inscription honoring her bravery in saving Fort Davis. Legend or fact?

* * * * *

Georgetown is the "Red Poppy Capital of Texas," so named by legislature and local residents. Georgetown is supposed to be the only location in the country where red poppies reseed themselves year after year. The story goes that Henry Purl "Okra" Compton collected seeds in Europe during World War I and brought them home to his mother in Georgetown. It is felt that the majority of the area poppies are descended from these first seeds. Did you know that the red poppy is the emblem of the American Legion? And in case there is any question, these are not the kind of poppies grown for opium and are entirely legal.

* * * * *

Did you know that **Gladewater** has the world's richest self-supporting cemetery? No, you didn't read it wrong. The Rosedale Cemetery was started in 1856. In 1932 two oil wells were drilled on the cemetery's land but away from the graves. The Gladewater Cemetery Association signed a contract for the drilling rights and royalties, and all money received goes for the upkeep of the cemetery. No living person can touch the money. The Gladewater Cemetery Association could enter into such an agreement since they sold permits for burial and retained all surface and mineral rights. The two wells were plugged in January of 1973, but until that time, the dead had a monthly income to maintain their beautiful resting place.

* * * * *

Groves was a rice farming community around the early 1900s. About this time, some of the area farmers got together and drilled a water well where the elementary school is located today. It was very disappointing because instead of hitting water, they hit oil at 800 feet! Not looking for oil, the group capped the well and went elsewhere to look for water! Had the group realized what they had, Groves could have had the history of Spindletop instead of Beaumont.

* * * * *

General Granberry, whom **Granbury** was named after, practiced law in Waco and in Seguin. He died in the Battle of Franklin and was buried in Columbia, Tennessee. A new burial site was prepared for the general in Granbury, and it was arranged for his remains to be sent for burial, but he arrived before the site was ready. A place was prepared at the bank, and General Granberry spent the next two years in the vault awaiting the preparation of his final resting place and burial in 1893.

* * * * *

Did you know **Jesse James** died in Granbury at the age of 107 and was buried in the Granbury Cemetery in 1951? The story is told that Jesse James' death was faked in 1882. Actually, a gentlemen by the name of Charlie Bigelow was the man shot, or so it is claimed. Mr. Bigelow would pass himself off as the famous James, so when he was shot, he took on the identity so Jesse could live out his life quietly.

* * * * *

Did you know that in the 1920s and 1930s the state held **annual rat killing campaigns**? The rats were ruining the stored crops. The school children were the ones that the state sent after the rats, and local merchants gave prizes for the most rats killed—verified by the number of tails that were turned in. According to a story in the December 1929 *Greenville Messenger*, the Floyd School was reported to have 1200 tails to date—wonder what the state count was?

* * * * *

Legend tells of the outlaw **Bill Longley**, who killed 32 men, being hanged three different times and living to escape to Mexico. The people of Giddings think differently. Bill Longley was hanged in Giddings on October 11, 1878 and buried there, or so they say. Fact or legend—which do you choose to believe?

* * * * *

Hereford was once known as "The Town Without A Toothache." Seems the natural fluoride in the water coupled with the minerals in the homegrown food kept the tooth decay rate very low. Dr. George Heard discovered the lack of tooth decay when he moved his dental practice to Hereford in 1905. He spoke several times to the dental society about his findings and how he felt that it was the diet of the local people. None of the other dentists seemed interested until Dr. Edward Taylor, from the dental section of the Texas Health Department, came to follow up on Dr. Heard's studies. Dr. Taylor's studies verified Dr. Heard's theory and probably led to the addition of fluoride to public water supplies and its addition to toothpaste.

* * * * *

Staggers Point got its name when a wagon train with Irish Protestants, who liked their Irish whiskey, staggered to that point and said, "This is as far as we go." . . . . . hmmmm.

* * * * *

Looking for buried treasure? Legend tells of a gentleman named Trammell, who was part of pirate Jean LaFitte's outfit, passing through the area today known as **Hughes Springs**. The trail he took is now named after him, Trammell Trace. Before he was killed by Indians, he was supposed to have buried several packhorse loads of treasure.

* * * * *

When you go to **Hondo**, notice the sign greeting you:

THIS IS GOD'S COUNTRY
PLEASE DON'T
DRIVE THROUGH IT
LIKE HELL

The sign has been there since 1930, proposed as a joke to slow down speeding cars coming through town. Only once did the sign come down, in the 1940s—because of objections to one of the words. A change was made to the sign—the word please was added—and the sign was once again put up!

* * * * *

Iraan is the combination of two names, Ira and Ann, Yates that is. In 1927 a contest was held to select a name for the new town with the first prize being a choice lot in town. The Yates submitted the winning entry, and thus the name Iraan.

* * * * *

During the 1930s, people came to **Italy** from all over to see the serpent-like creature that was reported to be in the creek bottoms south of town. The creature was featured in the news all over the country and was supposed to be like the Loch Ness Monster. The sighting of a colony of long-tailed rabbits in the area were also stirring up quite a bit of interest. Italy, fact or fiction?

* * * * *

The county of **Karnes** was named after Henry Wax Karnes, a scout and a Texas Ranger. Karnes had bright red hair, and there is a story about how his hair saved him from death. He was captured by Indians, and they wanted to know what he put on his hair to make it so red. They were not convinced when he told them it was natural and promptly took him to the San Antonio River to wash out the "berry juice" or whatever was causing the color. When the red would not come out, the Indians let him go, thinking he was some kind of god.

* * * * *

The hurricane of 1900, that destroyed most of Galveston Island, also destroyed **Katy**. There were only two buildings in Katy that were not damaged in any way, the homes of J.H. Wright and Mr. Featherston. No one knows why the storm "passed over them."

* * * * *

Colonel John Jacob Myers of **Lockhart** was one of the best known trail drivers during the late 1800s. He drove four to sixteen thousand head of cattle to Abilene, Kansas, annually. Even though he faced dangers all the time he drove cattle, his death was not the result of a cattle drive accident. Coming back home from a drive up in Utah,

Colonel Myers was robbed and chloroformed. He did manage to make it home to Lockhart before dying from chloroform poisoning in 1874.

* * * * *

Angelina County is the only county in Texas to be named after a woman. Angelina, meaning "little angel," was the name given to an Indian girl by Franciscan monks who explored the East Texas area. Angelina studied with the monks and learned the Spanish language. The French explorer St. Denis used Angelina as an interpreter. St. Denis founded Natchitoches, Louisiana, and the Catholic church records an Indian girl by the name of Angelina, buried in that town. In addition to the county, her name was given to a river, village, and a national forest.

* * * * *

In 1913 an explosion totally demolished the train depot in **Lufkin**. The station master's body was never found in the rubble. After a few of the townspeople thought his body could have been blown up into the standpipe behind the depot, the 100-foot standpipe was drained, but still no body. At this point they started suspecting the absent station master of blowing up the depot and quit looking for his body.

* * * * *

In August of 1902 a major fire destroyed every building in **Livingston**, between Abbey and Polk streets, except the brick courthouse. A man was accused of burning down the town, but his trial in Livingston ended in a hung jury, and his new trial in Huntsville cleared him of the charges. Seems the man was in the illegal liquor business, and he was at odds with the prohibitionists. Livingston still does not allow any legal sales of intoxicating liquors.

* * * * *

There is a story that around 1857 or 1858 the stage passed **Jacksboro** by about three or four miles to the south. To entice the stage to stop, a good road was built to intersect the Butterfield Trail, but the stage still took its old route. Several unnamed men from Jacksboro and Jack County met one dark night on the old stage trail where the stage went through a narrow pass in a cliff. The men blocked the road with huge boulders and completely blocked the stage's path. Guess what? The next run of the Butterfield stage stopped in Jacksboro!

* * * * *

Memphis decided in its early years that it needed a train stop and a depot for its growing town. In order to get the train to stop in Memphis, the tracks were greased! The culprits aren't known, but they accomplished what they set out to do—it was impossible for the train to move!

* * * * *

The original name of **Mercedes** was Diaz, named after the president of Mexico at the time. Sensing an uprising against the Diaz government in the Republic of Mexico, the town's name was changed to Mercedes, after Mercedes Diaz, the president's wife.

* * * * *

An Indian legend tells of the chief of the Caddos having a vision in 1811. The chief was warned to take his people to higher ground, and once they reached the safe area, the ground began to tremble. Where the tribe once lived, the ground sank and floods filled the land, the area now called **Caddo Lake**. Caddo Lake was once a chain of smaller lakes that were connected during the quake. Historians call this the great New Madrid earthquake. It was supposed to have shaken all of the Southern states. Caddo is now the largest natural lake in the South with an average depth of less than 10 feet.

* * * * *

Roberts County saw an election in 1889 to organize the county, but the election was invalidated because of illegal voting practices. This did not stop the "elected officials" from opening a courthouse in a vacant store in Miami and putting the records in a safe with a combination lock. The legally elected officials later obtained the records by hiring a gunman to pose as a landowner and take the records when the safe was opened!

* * * * *

Mineola was called **Sodom** before 1873. In 1873 two railroad lines were headed for the town of Sodom, the Texas & Pacific and the International & Great Northern Railway. The two railroad company heads agreed that whoever reached Sodom first would win crossing rights and would own the terminal property. The Texas & Pacific employed convict labor and the International & Great Northern used free labor. On May 23, 1873, The International & Great Northern won the race by about 15 minutes.

* * * * *

Legend tells of a Caddo Indian Chief in the Sabine River area that had twin sons; one was blonde and fair skinned, named Nacagdoches, and one had dark hair and skin, named Natchitoches. Just before the chief died, he gave them instructions that upon his death, each son would take his family on a three-day journey in different directions. Nacogdoches was to travel to the setting sun and Natchitoches was to travel to the rising sun. The area around Nacogdoches was settled by the blonde-haired tribe and the dark-haired brother established his tribe in the area around Natchitoches, Louisiana. The two tribes carved out a well-traveled trade route between them that is part of what became known as **El Camino Real**, often called the Old San Antonio Road.

* * * * *

William Goyens was the only Negro to be granted a State of Texas Centennial marker at his grave. Goyens was born a slave in South Carolina in 1794 and came to Texas in 1821. He was an Indian Agent and lawyer under the Mexican government in Texas. He participated in the Texas Revolution in 1836 and was an interpreter for a treaty with the Cherokee Indians in 1836. The Constitution of the Republic of Texas and of the State of Texas prohibited blacks from owning land, but at the time of his death in 1856, Goyens owned thousands of acres of land. He was noted for his charity and gifts.

* * * * *

On March 28, 1937, an explosion at the **New London** school killed over 400 people—the exact number varies with different accounts of the horrible event. Seems the school tapped on to a "wet" gas line, an oilfield byproduct, to save money on heating costs, without the permission of the gas company. A spark from an electric switch ignited leaking gas from faulty connections, which resulted in the mass death and destruction.

* * * * *

There is a story about some oil people who came to Balmorhea from Oklahoma in the early 1930s. They stayed in the area for several weeks enjoying the area and the people. The local people noticed that they liked to do strange things, such as shooting at cans in the air, throwing hand grenades, and jumping on and off the running boards of moving cars, but they didn't question their actions. Several months after the group left, the news came from Chicago that Public Enemy No. 1 had been killed. Because of the writeup and the description, the people of Balmorhea realized that their Oklahoma oil visitors were really the **John Dillinger Gang**!

* * * * *

The first murder in **Ector County** was that of a Chinese cook. A cowboy that was refused a meal shot the cook, but at the trial he was released after the judge ruled that no law existed against killing a Chinaman. The date of the incident is unknown.

* * * * *

One story about **"Bigfoot" Wallace**, an Indian fighter and Texas Ranger, says that he called his knife "Butch" and his gun "Sweetlips."

* * * * *

There is a story about **Governor Hogg** as a boy going to the courthouse to find the sheriff in trouble. The men, who would have killed the sheriff, were mad because James Hogg showed up and spoiled their plans. One of the outlaws shot Hogg and left him for dead. This was in 1869, and in 1891 he became the first native Texan to become governor.

* * * * *

In Hardman County there are four hills about 350 feet above the surrounding area called **Medicine Mounds**. The mounds are in a line, but the tallest has a flat cap rock on top. The Indians believed that this was the dwelling place of a powerful spirit. The legend is told of a medicine man whose daughter was very ill, but he could not cure her. As she grew worse, a spirit told him to take his medicines to the highest of the mounds and mix them there, which he did. He returned, giving his daughter the medicine, and she recovered. After this miracle was told, the medicine men paid visits to the mountain to receive its powers. This is how the four mounds became the Medicine Mounds.

* * * * *

Quanah is named for the great **Comanche Indian Chief Quanah Parker**. Quanah's mother was Cynthia Ann Parker, a white woman who had been captured when she was nine during a raid on Parker's Fort in 1836. The only one of five captives that was not recovered,

Cynthia grew up with the Indians and was called Naduah, meaning "she carries herself with dignity and grace." Naduah married Chief Peta Nocona and had three children, Quanah being the oldest. In December 1860, Sul Ross and his Texas Rangers raided the village and captured Cynthia and her daughter, Prairie Flower. They were returned to their family in East Texas. Prairie Flower died, and six months after the baby's death, in October 1864, Cynthia died. Legend says she died of a broken heart—the captivity of the civilized world was too much for someone who had grown up with and loved the free life of the Comanche people.

* * * * *

At one time **Comanche Chief Quanah Parker** had six wives. When he became "civilized," he was told he could only have one wife and must tell the others to leave, at which he replied, "You tell 'em."

* * * * *

A story is told about an Indian incident near **Linnville**. Several of the town folk were escaping from the Indians to a nearby boat when a Mrs. Watts remembered a watch she left behind. Mr. and Mrs. Watts returned only to have the Indians kill Mr. Watts and capture Mrs. Watts. A posse caught the Indians but Mrs. Watts had been shot with an arrow. Luck must have been with her that day, the arrow was deflected by a steel stay in her corset!

* * * * *

In an effort to find oil, gas, or minerals on his land, **C. W. Post** brought in an oil driller and crew in September 1910. After hitting granite in March 1911 the well was abandoned. A second well begun in April 1911 was drilled to a depth of 1,712 feet by January 1912. The crew lost the drill rod and this well was also abandoned. An interesting fact is that had the crew gone down another 300 feet they would have hit the oil that Mr. Post was looking for! Oil was discovered in the same spot twenty years later.

* * * * *

The first election of **Garza County** officials was held at the O.S. Ranch. A total of 75 ballots were required to make everything legal. Legend tells of the horses voting to make up the required number of ballots!

* * * * *

Chapter 1

On March 22 of each year residents of **Post** gather for an Indian ceremony called Taba'na Yuan'e, or Sunrise Wind. According to legend, the direction of the wind at sunrise on March 22, the day after spring begins, tells what kind of a year it will be. A wind out of the east or northeast means a very good year, a north or northwest wind is an average year, west and southwest is a poor year, and south or southeast wind predicts a very bad year. You may not believe the legend, but records starting with 1906 show the predictions to be 92% accurate!

* * * * *

Copano Bay, it is told, was used by the pirate Jean LaFitte as a base of operations at one time. Legend also has some of his stolen treasures buried on the shores of Copano Bay.

* * * * *

Temple is known as the "City of Trees" because of Mr. Goodrich Jones. Noting the lack of trees, he started a movement to plant trees all over town. The town hired men to dig up hackberry trees down at the river and replant them in town. Mr. Jones and a group of citizens requested that the state establish an "Arbor Day" in 1899, a day set aside to plant trees each year. This was the nation's first Arbor Day and Mr. Jones became the father of Arbor Day.

* * * * *

There is a legend of a **lost gold mine** in the Guadalupe Mountains. A gentleman by the name of Charles Dixon tried to find the gold after his Mescalaro sweetheart told him of its location. Mr. Dixon never found the mine, but in 1892 another man, by the name of Mr. Sublet, brought gold nuggets into Midland describing the place where he found them. The description fit the mine in the legend, but before anyone could get the exact location, Sublet died.

* * * * *

Wilbarger County is named after **Josiah Wilbarger** who came to Texas in 1830. Wilbarger was a member of a five-party scouting expedition in 1833 that was attacked by Indians. Two men of the party and Wilbarger were seriously injured. As Wilbarger lay dying, an Indian took his scalp. The Indian did not cut his throat since he thought he was already dead. Two of the other members of the party did escape but turned as they were leaving to see about 50 Indians swarm over the three injured men. Wilbarger managed to hold on to life when he saw a vision of his sister telling him to stay put and his friends would soon come to get him. The vision of his sister faded in the direction of a friend's house. Later, the two men who escaped made it to safety, telling of the murder of the others. There was no reason to go out to look for them since they were obviously dead, but during the night, one of the wives saw a vision of Wilbarger sitting under a tree alive and woke the men telling them to go out and look for him. The men did find Wilbarger just as was described, alive and under a tree. Later, Mrs. Hornsby, who had had the vision, told Wilbarger, and he told her of the vision of his sister encouraging him to hang on, that help was on the way. During his recuperation, Wilbarger received a letter telling of his sister's death one day before his ordeal. He always covered his head with a fur cap and told the story many times. He finally died from an accidental blow to his exposed skull.

* * * * *

The community of **Egypt** was named after the story in the Bible about the people coming for food. In 1827 a general drought affected the area around Egypt, but Egypt was blessed with rain and abundant corn. The people from Austin's colony came to the area for the corn, saying they were "going down into Egypt for corn," and the community's name took hold.

* * * * *

One of the local legends around **Waxahachie** is about the faces carved on the courthouse. The building was built in 1896 with Burnet County red granite, and three sculptors were brought from Italy to do the intricate carving on the stones. One of the men, Harry Hurley, fell in love with the young daughter of the lady who ran the boarding house where he was staying. Mr. Hurley carved a beautiful likeness of the young woman, Mable Frame, in the arch of the east entrance of the courthouse. When the young woman and her mother discouraged Mr. Hurley's courting, the other facial carvings on the courthouse began taking a different appearance—not so attractive. There are other young women's faces, possibly other women in Ellis County or Mr. Hurley's new way of seeing Miss Frame. There are faces of men on the courthouse also, but most are disagreeable looking, one with a droopy mustache, and one is the likeness of a devil. Is this really the way the three sculptors saw the people of the area, or just the ones they took a dislike to?

* * * * *

Did you know that there are supposed to be **three ghosts** at the Catfish Plantation Restaurant in Waxahachie? The ghosts are of two women and one man who lived in the old home in years past. The phenomena has been researched by professionals and believed to be real. The owners of the restaurant aren't afraid since the ghosts seem to be very friendly and don't appear on a daily basis. Why not go sample the catfish and get the whole story from the source?

* * * * *

There is a legend about "Lover's Leap," a high cliff over the Bosque River near **Waco**. Indian legend tells of a young Huaco Indian girl and an Apache brave who met and fell in love. Their union would not be permitted since their tribes were at war with each other. They decided to run away, but the girl's father followed the couple down the banks of the Bosque River with a group of Huaco warriors. Seeing that the situation was hopeless, they held each other and dove off the cliff to their deaths.

* * * * *

There is a story about **Police Marshal Robert Bailey** of West in the 1930s. The chief was nicknamed "High Pockets" since he stood 6 foot 7 inches tall, probably the tallest law officer in Texas at the time. His wife was 4 foot 11 inches! Anyway, seems that for the safety of the community, Chief Bailey tested the quality of every batch of moonshine sold on the local market. Even during prohibition, the only place you couldn't buy whiskey was the post office. When the federal officials came to town, Chief Bailey warned the storekeepers. He was a good chief, looking out for the townspeople, serving them over 25 years; he just had a different outlook on some things.

* * * * *

The **Canton-Wills Point War** started in 1877 when Wills Point decided it was a better place for the county seat than Canton was. Canton had been the county seat of Van Zandt County since 1851. An election was held in 1877 to determine the location of the new county seat, and when the votes from Canton and Alsa were thrown out because of irregularities, Wills Point won the election. Wills

Point formed a calvary and an infantry unit to take the records from Canton. Armed citizens brought the records back to Canton, and the whole dispute went to the Texas Supreme Court. Its decision placed the county seat right back in Canton. In the meantime, Canton people needed a trading place, and since they did not want to have anything to do with Wills Point, the little town of Edgewood developed.

* * * * *

Believe in ghosts? Legend claims that the **New Birmingham Trail** is haunted. The trail is only a 2.6 mile walking trail that follows a route that in the 1880s was a major connection between New Birmingham and the rest of Texas. New Birmingham no longer exists, but it was located southeast of Rusk.

* * * * *

Legends of a **lost silver mine** are still told in the Menard area.

* * * * *

There is a legend about a man named John St. John who tended bar in Granbury in Hood County. When Mr. St. John died, in Somervell County, on his deathbed he confessed to being **John Wilkes Booth**. Truth or legend? Not many men confess to something like this on their deathbeds—or do they?

* * * * *

Oliver Loving, called the "Dean of Texas Trail Drivers," was the founder of three major cattle trails with his partner, Charles Goodnight. He died of complications of wounds from an Indian attack on a drive in New Mexico. He died on September 25, 1867 and was buried in New Mexico, but his dying wish was to be taken back to Texas. His son, Joseph, and Charles Goodnight brought Loving's body back to Texas in March of 1868 for burial in the Greenwood Cemetery in Weatherford.

* * * * *

Braggin' Rights

Texas State Capitol Building—Austin, Texas

The dome of the **Capitol in Austin** is seven feet higher than the dome on the Capitol in Washington, D.C.

＊ ＊ ＊ ＊ ＊

Round Top is the smallest incorporated town in the state of Texas. Population of Round Top is 81 and only 1 square mile in area.

＊ ＊ ＊ ＊ ＊

The **Shelby County courthouse**, built in 1885, was designed by Jacob Joseph Emmett Gibson to look like a castle from his native Ireland. Just like a castle, the courthouse has its own secret passage-way—for the presiding judge to escape after giving an unpopular decision! It is the only one of its kind in the U.S.

＊ ＊ ＊ ＊ ＊

Stafford Municipal School District is the only municipal school district in Texas. The 1992-93 school year was their tenth year in operation. The system and the city enjoy shared facilities and services such as a joint maintenance and transportation center, and the Stafford Civic Center is available for school functions. With the problems that Texas is facing with our schools and funding today, perhaps we should all take a closer look at the Stafford Municipal School District.

＊ ＊ ＊ ＊ ＊

The **Morton Salt mine** in Grand Saline is one of only three in the U.S. to be a continuous supplier of rock salt. You cannot tour the salt mine but you can visit the Salt Palace, the only building in the world bricked with salt.

＊ ＊ ＊ ＊ ＊

The first motorized fire truck in the state of Texas was purchased by the city of **Big Spring** in 1909.

＊ ＊ ＊ ＊ ＊

The original sculpture used in casting the bronzed Marine Corps Memorial in Arlington, Virginia, is in **Harlingen** on the Marine Military Academy campus. The sculpture, 102 feet tall and weighing 130 tons, immortalizes the raising of the U.S. flag over Iwo Jima during World War II.

＊ ＊ ＊ ＊ ＊

Marathon had a processing plant, built in 1907 and operating until around 1926, that produced raw, natural rubber from the guayule plant. This processing plant was the first and only plant of its kind in the country. The guayule plant grows wild in the Big Bend area.

* * * * *

Texas' first highway roadside park is 10 miles west of **La Grange**.

* * * * *

David Wayne Hooks Airport in **Tomball** is the state's largest privately owned airport.

* * * * *

The **first glass factory** in Texas was established in Three Rivers in 1913.

* * * * *

In 1870 a 474-foot-long **suspension bridge** was built in Waco across the Brazos River for people and cattle to cross. When the bridge was built, it was the longest single span suspension bridge in the world. The company that oversaw the building of the bridge later oversaw the building of the Brooklyn Bridge. Yes, ours was first! For twenty years after its completion, the bridge was a toll bridge. Today the bridge is only open to foot traffic.

* * * * *

The **world's largest strawberry**—or at least a replica—stands seven feet tall, weighs 1600 pounds, and can be found in Poteet. Poteet produces 40% of Texas' strawberries and decided to honor the fruit with its own monument.

* * * * *

Texas' **first newspaper** was published in Nacogdoches. The newspaper's name was *Gaceta de Tejas*.

* * * * *

In 1873 the world's **first ammonia refrigerant ice plant** was built in Jefferson.

* * * * *

The world's **largest jackrabbit** stands 10 feet tall and is located in the school administration parking lot in Odessa.

* * * * *

The first Polish school in the United States was in Panna Maria. Panna Maria, meaning Virgin Mary in Polish, is believed to be the **oldest Polish settlement** in America.

* * * * *

The world's **largest grapefruit juice canning plant** is in Weslaco.

* * * * *

San Antonio has five military bases, more than any other city in America.

* * * * *

A huge live oak tree, estimated to be 2000 years old and certified as the largest in Texas, is located in **Goose Island State Park** about 12 miles north of Rockport.

* * * * *

There were 72 World War II **prisoner of war** camps in Texas—more than any other state.

* * * * *

Wharton County is the largest **rice** producing county in the state.

* * * * *

The **Capitol in Austin** is the nation's largest statehouse.

* * * * *

Helium is found near Amarillo in the world's greatest quantity. In 1968 a six-story monument was erected to recognize this natural element. The stainless steel Helium Monument contains a 1,000-year time capsule.

* * * * *

Balmorhea State Park has one of the world's largest pools. The pool has a 62,000-square-foot surface and is spring fed. The springs put out 25 million gallons daily.

* * * * *

On the courthouse square in **Seguin** is a five-foot-long, 1000-pound pecan made of metal and plaster—probably the world's largest.

* * * * *

The Smith-Hoyt-Youngs House, in **Atlanta,** was built in 1887 and claims to have had the first indoor bath and the first telephone in town.

* * * * *

The *Bastrop Advertiser*, established in 1853, is the **oldest weekly newspaper** in Texas.

* * * * *

Dallas is the Southwest's largest banking center.

* * * * *

Billy Bob's Texas, in Fort Worth, is the world's **largest honky-tonk** and includes a 4800-square-foot rodeo arena.

* * * * *

Galveston had the **first electric lights** in the state.

* * * * *

Galveston was the site of the **first medical college** in the state.

* * * * *

A mantel, in the **Bishop's Palace** in Galveston, was awarded first prize at the 1876 Philadelphia World's Fair.

* * * * *

Houston is the largest city in Texas, and it is one of the nation's largest seaports.

* * * * *

Laredo is the nation's largest inland port.

* * * * *

Dyess Air Force Base, in Abilene, is the home of the B-1B bomber, and the only training center for its crew.

* * * * *

The city of **Azle** was called O-Bar, but it was changed in 1883 in honor of Dr. Azle Steward who deeded the land for the townsite. What makes the name Azle special is the fact that there is no other post office in the United States by that name.

* * * * *

Fort Hood, located about 18 miles from Belton, is the largest armored military installation in the free world.

* * * * *

The Hoechst Celanese Corp. in Bishop has branched out into the production of bulk pharmaceuticals and has a new ibuprofen unit. Completed in 1992, it is the world's largest **ibuprofen** production center.

* * * * *

The oldest German band in the country, or the world outside of Germany, is the **Boerne Village Band**. They have been playing true German music for 132 consecutive years. If you want to see the band, they often have open free concerts at the Boerne Main Plaza. So contact the Chamber of Commerce for dates and bring a blanket to sit on the lawn and enjoy a special evening.

* * * * *

The first **cross-country airplane flight** was made from Ft. Sam Houston to Leon Springs in 1911. The round trip was 26 miles and was made in 1 hour and 45 minutes.

* * * * *

Did you know that **Borger** has one of the longest main streets in the country?

* * * * *

The only **graphite mine** in the southern U.S. is located on Graphite Mine Road, along the eastern shore of Lake Buchanan, west of Burnet.

* * * * *

The **Veterans Memorial Bridge**, the sister to the Rainbow Bridge built in 1938, was completed in 1990, with a clearance of only 143 feet above the Neches, and is the first cable-stayed suspension bridge in Texas. The two bridges connect Bridge City and Port Arthur.

* * * * *

Blinn College was founded in 1883 in Brenham, with only three students in the Mission Institute, and became the first county-owned junior college in Texas.

* * * * *

The **Washington County Fair** is the oldest county fair in Texas. The 125th annual festival was celebrated in September 1993.

* * * * *

Coggin Academy's McClelland Library, in **Brownwood,** is the oldest educational building still in use in the state of Texas. It was built in 1876.

* * * * *

In the spring of 1872, the last division of the International & Great Northern Railroad was completed, linking Hearne to Palestine, making this the **longest railroad** in the U.S. entirely within one state.

* * * * *

Each April the Junior League sponsors the World's Largest Garage Sale in the **Arlington** Community Center. The center is 24,000 square feet—must be a VERY big garage sale!

* * * * *

Amarillo Little Theatre, in **Amarillo,** is the longest continuously performing little theatre in the U.S.

* * * * *

The first 4th of July celebration in Texas was at **Beason's,** now Columbus, in 1826, celebrating the 50th anniversary of the U.S.

* * * * *

Did you know the **oldest home** in Texas is supposed to be in Wheelock?

* * * * *

Tyler is the Rose Capital of Texas.

* * * * *

Comanche's estimated deer population is 14,900. The turkey population is estimated at 5,514. A tom turkey killed in **Comanche** in 1985 had a 15-inch beard—a world record, and a 26-pound tom was killed in the spring of 1986, which is being confirmed as a world record weight.

* * * * *

The oldest original existing courthouse in Texas is in Comanche. **Old Cora**, as she is called, was built in 1856 and moved to her present location in Comanche in 1984. Old Cora was in the town of Cora which was the county seat of Comanche County at the time.

* * * * *

A **water oak** located on the Lawson Farm in Shelby County became the Texas Champion in 1960 and the National Champion until 1973, when it died. The tree was 253 1/2 inches around, was 77 feet tall, and had a crown spread of 104 feet.

* * * * *

The Texas Safari, in Clifton, is supposed to be the world's largest **exotic animal drive-through reserve.** In the grizzly bear compound be sure to look for Ben, the star of "Grizzly Adams."

* * * * *

The **boundary line marker,** erected in 1840 by surveyors representing the United States of America and the Republic of Texas, marked the boundary between the Republic of Texas and Louisiana. It is the only boundary of its kind in the world, because it marked the boundary between two countries that now are within the U.S.

* * * * *

The **first automobile** made in Texas was made in Cleburne.

* * * * *

The Kendrick Religious Diorama & Museum, located between Eastland and Cisco, is Texas' only all **religious diorama museum**. The museum took 10 years to build and contains 140 life-size, realistic figures to give you the feeling of being there. The Kendrick Religious Pageant, rated as being the best outdoor drama in the state, covers the life of Christ from His birth through His resurrection, with productions at Easter and during the summer each Thursday and Friday from mid-June to mid-August.

* * * * *

Crane, the county seat of Crane County, is the only town in the 796-square-mile county. Crane also has the only post office in the county!

* * * * *

The largest U.S. collection of **Hakata dolls** is in the Museum of Oriental Cultures in Corpus Christi. They also have a 5-foot-tall bronze Buddha in their collection.

* * * * *

Mission Espiritu Santo and Presidio La Bahia were both established in 1749. These two make up the only Spanish Colonial fort-mission complex left standing in the Western Hemisphere. The Presidio is the only Texas Revolution site which retains its original 1836 appearance. These are located in **Goliad**.

* * * * *

Fort Hood, located about 18 miles from Belton, is a 339-square-mile installation—the **largest armored military installation** in the free world. It is the only post in the U.S. that has the capability to support two full divisions.

* * * * *

The world's **largest commissary** is located on the base at Fort Hood. The largest main retail store in the U.S. is also located there, The Main Exchange Shopping Complex.

* * * * *

The **highest bridge** in the state is just past the town of Comstock off of Highway 90. The bridge rises 273 feet above the bed of the Pecos River.

* * * * *

Lake Amistad is the third largest international man-made lake in the world. Amistad, by the way, means friendship in Spanish.

* * * * *

Val Verde Winery, established in 1883 in Del Rio, is the oldest bonded winery in Texas. Members of the Qualia family established the winery and have operated it continuously. The state of Texas has awarded the winery the Land Heritage Award from the Department of Agriculture for single-family ownership for over 100 years.

* * * * *

Garner State Park in Uvalde County is the most attended state park in Texas.

* * * * *

The Dallas/Fort Worth International Airport is located midway between the two cities and is the second busiest passenger airport in the world. In 1991, 48 million passengers went through **D/FW Airport**. D/FW offers 2000 daily flights to 1478 domestic and 35 international destinations.

* * * * *

Comanche Peak Steam Electric Station in Granbury is the **first nuclear power plant** in Texas.

* * * * *

The world's largest equestrian sculpture is The Mustangs of Las Colinas in **Las Colinas** in Irving. The sculpture is nine bronze mustangs crossing a granite stream. Las Colinas is a 12,000-acre business/residential development.

* * * * *

Denison had the **first ice factory** in North Texas in 1876.

* * * * *

Dublin adopted an official flag for the city on August 2, 1938, believed to be the only city in Texas with a special flag at that time. The flag has a green background with a white shamrock and white lettering, "Dublin, Texas," designed by the local Boy Scouts.

* * * * *

Texas Woman's University, founded in Denton in 1902, started out as the Girls Industrial Institute and College of Texas. Texas Woman's University is the largest women's university in the country.

* * * * *

The **first county** created under the Republic of Texas was Houston County.

* * * * *

Indian Mound Nursery in Alto is the only **state owned nursery**.

* * * * *

The first oil refinery in Texas was at **Corsicana**. The refinery was built in 1897 by Magnolia, the parent company of Mobil Oil. Corsicana is where Mobil Oil got its start.

* * * * *

The largest manufacturer of red clay pots in America is The Original Marshall Pottery in **Marshall**. They have been in business since 1895.

* * * * *

The **Sabine River** has the largest water discharge at its mouth of any Texas river—6.8 million acre feet. The name Sabine comes from the Spanish word for cypress.

* * * * *

El Paso is home to the Tiguas, Texas' oldest Indian tribe. The **Tigua Indians** are the oldest identifiable ethnic group in Texas.

* * * * *

Fredericksburg holds the oldest continuing county fair in Texas, the Gillespie County Fair, in August.

* * * * *

Gillespie County is the top peach producing county in the state.

* * * * *

Fort Martin Scott, two miles east of Fredericksburg, was the first frontier military fort in Texas, established in 1848. The fort was operational for only five years. The site was reopened in 1989 after some reconstruction; however, the stockade is original.

* * * * *

The Ashbel Smith Building, affectionately known as **"Old Red,"** at the University of Texas Medical Branch, at Galveston, is recognized as the oldest medical school building west of the Mississippi River.

* * * * *

The University of Texas Medical Branch in Galveston is Texas' **oldest and largest medical school**.

* * * * *

The 10 miles of continuous sidewalk on top of the seawall in Galveston is the longest skate boarding/roller skate track in the state—actually one of the world's **longest sidewalks**.

* * * * *

The **Flagship Hotel** on Seawall Blvd., in Galveston, is the only hotel in North America built entirely over the water.

* * * * *

Georgetown is the location of **Southwestern University**. Chartered in 1840, the university is the oldest institution of higher learning in Texas.

* * * * *

Granbury's old town square was the first in Texas to be listed in the National Register of Historic Places.

* * * * *

The first city in Texas to own and operate its own electric light plant was **Greenville**. Opened in 1891, the plant is the oldest municipal plant in the state.

* * * * *

Did you know that Greenville had the largest inland **cotton compress** in the world around 1900 and that it still holds the record for the most bales compressed in a single day? The number? 2073!

* * * * *

The Deaf Smith County courthouse in Hereford was completed in 1911 and made of Georgia marble. It is the **only marble courthouse** in Texas.

* * * * *

Harlingen is the number one destination for winter tourists in Texas who stay over 30 days. And why shouldn't they; the average year-round temperature in Harlingen is 74 degrees!

* * * * *

The first Kiwanis clubhouse built in the country is in **Pharr**—built in 1928.

* * * * *

The Texas Department of Corrections is the third largest **prison system** in the nation.

* * * * *

Houston has the world's largest concentration of energy and petro-chemical companies.

* * * * *

The **Corn Club** was organized September 8, 1907, in Jacksboro, by Tom M. Marks. Later the club became known as the 4-H Club. Mr. Marks was the special county agent for Jack County. He tried to convince the local farmers to plant newly developed corn varieties, but with no luck. Mr. Marks then organized the club, distributed the new corn seed to the young farmers, and in 1908, the first county fair was held and the corn was exhibited. To see memorabilia of the Corn Club, go to the Jack County Museum.

* * * * *

Jewett was the first town in the United States to be governed entirely by women. This first began in 1920 with Mrs. Hattie Adkisson elected as mayor.

* * * * *

The practice of storing butane and propane in salt domes was first used in 1950 in the **Keystone Field** in Winkler County.

* * * * *

Did you know that there are only five pyramid shaped houses in the U.S. and **Kermit** has one?

* * * * *

The Astrodome in Houston was the **first domed stadium** in the country.

* * * * *

The Dr. Eugene Clark Library, on Main in Lockhart, is the oldest continuously used **library** in Texas—modeled after the Villa Rotunda in Vicenza, Italy. The library was built in 1899.

* * * * *

The **largest yaupon** tree on the North American continent is 46 inches in circumference and 32 feet high. The tree is located east of Devers in Liberty County.

* * * * *

The **Cass County Courthouse** is the oldest functional courthouse in Texas and is listed in the National Register of Historic Places.

* * * * *

The **Confederate Air Force and American Airpower Heritage Museum**, located at the Midland International Airport, has the world's largest and most complete collection of World War II aircraft that are still flyable. The museum has 145 planes and 20 are on display at all times—the plane display is changed four times a year. The museum also has more than 70,000 artifacts dealing with aviation and the war during the years 1939 and 1945.

* * * * *

The first building in Texas, built for the sole purpose of being a homemaking education facility, is the Lillian Keith Cottage in **Mineral Wells**.

* * * * *

The Houston and Texas Central, originally chartered in 1848 as the Galveston and Red River Railroad, is thought to be the **oldest rail line** in Texas.

* * * * *

Charles W. Stewart, from Navasota, was the first person to sign the **Declaration of Independence** from Mexico.

* * * * *

Oak Grove Cemetery, in Nacogdoches, is the site of the oldest marked grave in Texas, dated 1837.

* * * * *

The Comal River, going through New Braunfels, is the shortest U.S. river—2.5 miles long. The **Comal River** could be the shortest in the world; it is often referred to as such.

* * * * *

The **Petroleum Museum, Library and Hall of Fame**, in Midland, is the largest petroleum type museum in the world, with the largest collection of antique oilfield equipment.

* * * * *

On July 4, 1883 the world's **first rodeo** was held in Pecos.

* * * * *

The Alibates Flint Quarries National Monument, in the Panhandle in Potter County, is the **only national monument** in Texas. The monument consists of 1079 acres where for 10,000 years Indians dug for flint to make arrowheads, implement points, and other tools.

* * * * *

The World's First Championship **Jackrabbit Roping contest** was held during the 1932 Odessa Rodeo although with numerous objections. The contest was again held in 1977. Animal lovers delayed the contest by setting the rabbits free—except they came back at supper time, and the contest proceeded. The Humane Society blocked all future events of this contest with a court order in 1978.

* * * * *

The **first scientific excavation** in Texas was in 1907 in the Wolf Creek Valley near Perryton in Ochiltree County. Carbon dating shows the area was continuously inhabited until around A.D. 1500 and village ruins have been found in the area of over 20 different periods. This area and these sites are considered to be some of the most important prehistoric Indian sites in the country, according to archaeologists.

* * * * *

Somerset is known as one of the world's largest shallow oil fields.

* * * * *

The **Nickel Baptist Church** in Palestine was called that because it was built by the contribution of nickels around 1887. The church is the oldest church building in Palestine.

* * * * *

Kolstad's in Palestine was the first jewelry store west of the Mississippi. It is also the oldest retail firm in Texas, being here since 1853. The present location, since 1896, displays a chandelier weighing over 250 pounds, with 1200 pieces, each individually signed by Waterford in honor of Kolstad's 125th anniversary.

* * * * *

Did you know that the first Texas bank to reopen after the nationwide bank closing in the 1930s was Bonner & Robinson, Bankers, in **Palestine**? The Old Robinson Bank Building, built in 1890, is on Main Street.

* * * * *

The **Texas Travel Information Center** in the Valley is the state's busiest branch.

* * * * *

The **rope-pulled freight elevator** in the old Holman Hardware & Furniture building, built in 1893, is considered the oldest in Texas still in use. The hardware store is in downtown Pittsburg and now houses the Pittsburg Antiques Center.

* * * * *

Hurricane Beulah, in September of 1967, landed near Brownsville with winds clocked at 136 miles per hour. The hurricane spawned 115 tornadoes, which is the largest number on record for any hurricane.

* * * * *

The world's smallest Catholic church is a few miles south of **Round Top** on Texas 237.

* * * * *

The Morton Cemetery, in **Fort Bend,** is the final resting place of Robert Gillespie, whose grave is marked with the oldest Masonic monument in Texas.

* * * * *

The largest aluminum smelter in the country is in **Rockdale**.

* * * * *

The footbridge in **Rusk** was designed by Howard Barnes and is claimed to be the longest wooden trestle-type in the nation—546 feet long and 4 feet wide. The wooden footbridge, built in 1861, allowed the early citizens of the east valley to get to town when the creek flooded. The old footbridge was torn down in 1889 and a new one, designed by Mr. Barnes, built. Although the bridge has always been called "the footbridge," Mr. Barnes called it the Frazer Bridge on his notes. The bridge was maintained by the city until 1950 and restored in 1969 using the original plans of Mr. Barnes. The footbridge is located in the Footbridge Garden Park in Rusk.

* * * * *

Angelo State University has the largest **planetarium** in Texas, and it is the fourth largest university planetarium in the nation.

* * * * *

The Jerusalem C.M.E. Church in San Augustine is the **oldest black church** of record in Texas. Organized around 1845, the church was first known as the "Church on the Branch."

* * * * *

The grain elevators in **Saginaw**, owned by the Far-Mar-Co. since 1977, are the largest in the world. The elevators have a 28-million-bushel capacity.

* * * * *

San Augustine had Texas' **first Boy Scout troop**, organized by Rev. George F. Crocket.

* * * * *

Mission Concepcion, in San Antonio, is the **oldest unrestored church** in the nation.

* * * * *

Kaspar Wire Works in **Shiner** is the largest producer and renovator of newspaper racks in the nation. They also make wire baskets and other wire products. The company, founded in 1893, is still owned by the same family and employs around 900 people.

* * * * *

The **Spoetzl Brewery** was established in Shiner in 1909 with brewmaster Kosmos Spoetzl. The German and Czech farmers of the area wanted a beer that tasted like it came from the old country, so they sought out Spoetzl. The brewery is the last little brewery in Texas and has been in continuous operation since it opened. Its product is made, bought, and consumed entirely in Texas. The brewery's annual production is 25,000 barrels. It remained open during the prohibition period by making near-beer and ice. The Spoetzl Brewery is a Registered Texas Historical Landmark.

* * * * *

The Miguel Aleman Suspension Bridge is the only suspended bridge remaining on the **Rio Grande River**. The bridge, built in 1927, is located in Roma, Starr County.

* * * * *

The **Tyler Municipal Rose Garden** is the world's largest. Set on 22 acres, the 38,000 rose bushes represent 500 varieties of roses. The garden is believed to contain the most rose bushes of any formal rose garden in the world. The Texas Rose Festival was started in the 1930s, but roses were grown in the Tyler area commercially in 1870.

* * * * *

The Winton Gable All Faiths Chapel, located at the Terrell State Hospital, was opened in 1966 and was the **first chapel** in a state hospital in Texas. The chapel was built entirely from gifts, and not state funds, and seats 350 people. The Terrell State Hospital was established in 1885.

* * * * *

The **R.A. Terrell homeplace** is located on the campus of Southwestern Christian College in Terrell. It is special because it is one of only 20 remaining round houses in the U.S. The house has been designated a national landmark.

* * * * *

Port Lavaca has the "World's Longest Fishing Pier."

* * * * *

Piasano Pete, at Fort Stockton, is the "World's Largest Roadrunner," standing 10 feet tall and 22 feet long. The statue is one of the area's most photographed subjects.

* * * * *

The city of **Weimar** believes it had the first cotton oil mill in Texas, built around 1876.

* * * * *

The world's **largest sulphur dome**, the Boling Dome, is in Wharton County. Wharton County is said to have the largest known deposit of sulphur in the world.

* * * * *

The oldest natural history museum in Texas is the **Strecker Museum** on the Baylor University campus in Waco.

* * * * *

Lake Waco with 60 miles of shoreline is the largest urban lake in Texas.

* * * * *

The only State Meat Inspection Training School in Texas is located in **Yoakum**.

* * * * *

Sheppard Air Force Base in Wichita Falls is the headquarters for the Euro-NATO Joint Jet Pilot Training program, the only base in the world so chosen. Sheppard AFB is also one of the five largest technical training centers in the nation.

* * * * *

The **Heritage Village**, a collection of pioneer buildings and artifacts in Woodville, has the largest collection of East Texas historical artifacts in the state. Some of the buildings in the village are the post office, blacksmith's shop, syrup mill, railroad depot, apothecary shop, leather shop, log barn, little red schoolhouse, doctor's office, and of course the sheriff's office and justice of the peace.

* * * * *

Chapter 3 ———————————————

People and Places

Restored caboose used in Wills Point as the Hospitality Center by the Wills Point Historical Society. Located on Highway 80 in downtown Wills Point.

Blessing was so named when the Postal Service would not accept the name of the town as "Thank God."

* * * * *

The salt dome under **Grand Saline** could supply the world's salt needs for 20,000 years. The dome is approximately 1.5 miles across and 16,000 feet thick.

* * * * *

Texas A&M opened on October 4, 1876—with six students.

* * * * *

Want an example of Texas luck? When **Abilene** celebrated its centennial in 1981, they set up an oil drilling rig on the county fairgrounds to demonstrate the drilling process and, you guessed it, they struck oil. Enough for a small profitable production. Yep, Texas luck!

* * * * *

When Austin was chosen on January 19, 1840 as the site of the new capital of the Republic of Texas, it was called **Waterloo** and was occupied by only four families.

* * * * *

O'Donnell was the hometown of **Dan Blocker**—Hoss Cartwright to "Bonanza" fans.

* * * * *

A fragment of the genuine **Blarney Stone** from the ruins of Blarney Castle in Ireland is mounted in Elmore Park in Shamrock.

* * * * *

McLean was once known as the "uplift city" because of a ladies undergarment factory.

* * * * *

Brewster County is the largest county in Texas, with an area of 5,935 square miles. **Brewster County** is larger than the state of Connecticut.

* * * * *

Longhorn Cavern, in Longhorn Cavern State Park near Burnet, continues for two miles underground. The cave was the site of a secret gun powder manufacturer for the Confederate armies.

* * * * *

The **"Historic Oak"** on the north side of the La Grange square has been a favorite gathering spot for men during six different conflicts.

* * * * *

The **first governor** of the state of Texas was James Pinckney Henderson, who served from 1846 until 1847.

* * * * *

Anson Jones was the **last president** of Texas.

* * * * *

The **Georgia Monument** in Albany was erected in 1976 to fulfill a promise to honor the volunteer Georgia Battalion that fought for the state's independence in 1836. Most of the volunteers were killed at Goliad.

* * * * *

Texas seceded from the Union on January 28, 1861, and when **Governor Sam Houston** refused to pledge his allegiance to the Confederacy, he was removed from office.

* * * * *

The **battleship** *Texas* served as the flagship in the 1944 World War II D-Day invasion commanded by General Dwight D. Eisenhower. She is the only surviving naval vessel to have served in World Wars I & II. The ship is now permanently moored in the Houston Ship Channel at the San Jacinto Battleground State Historical Park.

* * * * *

On January 19, 1840, **Austin** was established as the site of the Texas Capitol.

* * * * *

The 1968 World's Fair—HemisFair '68—was held in **San Antonio** from April 6 to October 6, 1968. The fair was held on San Antonio's 250th anniversary.

* * * * *

The **"Archive War"** began March 10, 1842. This "war" was a dispute between Austin and Houston over the control of the State Archives.

* * * * *

The **cornerstone** to the Alamo's chapel was laid May 8, 1744.

* * * * *

After the **Battle of Nacogdoches** on August 2, 1832, Mexican troops were never again stationed in East Texas.

* * * * *

Camp Barkeley was a WW II army camp that housed over 60,000 men and was also a prisoner of war camp. The remains of the camp can be seen in Abilene.

* * * * *

The first man to die in the **Texas Revolution** was Richard Andrews, killed at the Battle of Concepcion, October 28, 1835.

* * * * *

Gonzales is referred to as the "**Lexington of Texas**" since the first shot of the Texas Revolution was fired here October 2, 1835. The Mexicans tried to take a cannon that was on loan to the Texans and we didn't want to give it up. The flag over the cannon read "Come and Take It." The Mexicans knew that trouble was brewing, and they were afraid that we would use the cannon, given for use against the Indians, against them—and they were right!

* * * * *

In 1840 Laredo was the capital of the Republic of the Rio Grande. The **Republic of the Rio Grande** consisted of the southwest Texas area and three northern Mexico states. The Republic of the Rio Grande was an uprising fighting for the restoration of state's rights, which Mexico defeated.

* * * * *

Did you know that **Marshall** was the Confederate capital of Missouri during the Civil War (1863—1865) and the Western Capital of the Confederacy after the fall of Vicksburg? Governor Reynolds selected Marshall to move to from Missouri because of the stagecoach line connections between St. Louis and Marshall.

* * * * *

There were survivors of the **Alamo** battle. Susanna Dickinson, wife of Captain Almeron Dickinson, and her daughter Angelina; Joe, Col. Travis' servant; Gertrudis Navarro, her sister Juana Navarro Alsbury, and her baby son Alijo (Gertrudis was the adopted sister of James Bowie's wife); Gregorio Esparza's wife, Ana, and her four children: Enrique, Francisco, Manuel, and Maria de Jesus; Trinidad Saucedo, and Petra Gonzales. Santa Anna allowed the women, children, and the others who did not fight, to live.

* * * * *

Palmito Hill Battlefield, east of Brownsville, was the site of the last land battle of the Civil War. The conflict took place May 12 and 13, 1865, more than a month after the South had surrendered. P.S. The South won this battle.

* * * * *

The first duly elected legislature of the **Republic of Texas** convened on October 3, 1836 in Columbia, the capital of Texas.

* * * * *

In 1837 Congress voted to move the capital from **Columbia** to Houston since Columbia did not seem to have enough room to house the governing body. Houston became the capital of Texas on April 19, 1837.

* * * * *

The grave of **Helena Kimble Dill** is located in Alto. She is believed to be the mother of the first Anglo child born in Texas. The child, born September 8, 1804, was also named Helena Dill. Jane Long of Galveston is often given credit for being the mother of the first Anglo child, born in 1821, but the title "Mother of Texas" really came as a result of her bravery during the period she was left defending a near empty fort at Point Bolivar near Galveston.

* * * * *

Sam Rayburn served as speaker of the U.S. House of Representatives longer than anyone else in American history. Tours through his home, in Bonham, can be taken hourly, but reservations are required for groups.

* * * * *

Sam Houston was born in Virginia, and his burial site is in Oakwood Cemetery in Houston.

* * * * *

Lady Bird Johnson, Mrs. LBJ, was **Claudia Taylor** before she married the former President. She was born in Karnack. Have you ever heard her called Claudia?

* * * * *

Sam Houston was a former governor of Tennessee.

* * * * *

Walter Williams is buried in Mount Pleasant Church Cemetery southeast of Franklin. Mr. Williams, a Confederate soldier, was the

last remaining veteran of the Civil War, both of the North and of the South.

＊ ＊ ＊ ＊ ＊

Protestant church services were unlawful in Texas in the early days since Mexico was **Catholic**. Sam Houston was even baptized a Catholic because Mexico required landholders to be Catholic.

＊ ＊ ＊ ＊ ＊

Colonel DeMorse was known as the "Father of Texas Journalism."

＊ ＊ ＊ ＊ ＊

O. Henry, the pen name of short story writer William Sydney Porter, lived in Austin from 1885 until 1895. His residence in Austin is open to visitors Wednesday through Sunday.

＊ ＊ ＊ ＊ ＊

Lyndon B. Johnson graduated from Southwest Texas State University in **San Marcos**.

＊ ＊ ＊ ＊ ＊

Both James Stephen Hogg and Thomas Mitchell Campbell were born in **Rusk**. Hogg was the first, and Campbell was the second native born governor of Texas.

＊ ＊ ＊ ＊ ＊

The Visitor's Center in **Granbury** is located in the old Hood County Jail built in 1885, complete with original cell block and hanging tower.

＊ ＊ ＊ ＊ ＊

The new **Texas State Aquarium** is located in Corpus Christi.

＊ ＊ ＊ ＊ ＊

In 1982 hundreds of **dinosaur tracks** were uncovered in Sattler. These tracks are believed to be made by a three-toed thunder lizard a hundred million years ago.

＊ ＊ ＊ ＊ ＊

How about a romantic horse-drawn surrey ride? **Jefferson** is full of history, and the surrey driver tells the city's story while you enjoy a 45-minute ride through the residential and business areas.

＊ ＊ ＊ ＊ ＊

The Thikol Chemical Corp. makes **rocket fuel** in Karnack.

＊ ＊ ＊ ＊ ＊

Van Zandt Gin Co., in **Wills Point,** started in 1891 and still operates during the fall cotton season.

* * * * *

Mineola is known as the "gateway to East Texas pine country."

* * * * *

Beginning in the spring with the bluebonnets and dogwoods and continuing through autumn and the brilliant fall foliage, Mineola welcomes visitors with their **Holiday Motor Trails**.

* * * * *

When **Saint Jo** was established in 1856, it was originally known as Head of Elm. Not so strange when you know that the town was established on the springs that were the headwaters of the Elm Fork of the Trinity River.

* * * * *

The city of **Zavalla** is within the Angelina National Forest.

* * * * *

The entire downtown square of **Llano** has been designated a National Historic District.

* * * * *

The state's largest railroad construction and repair shops are in **Cleburne**.

* * * * *

Denison was established in 1872 as a railhead for the first railroad coming into Texas from the north, the Missouri, Kansas & Texas.

* * * * *

In 1893 **Paducah** consisted of two stores, a schoolhouse, and a saloon that became the church on Sunday.

* * * * *

Ozona is the county seat of Crockett County—in fact, it is the *only* town in the whole county and the state's largest unincorporated town!

* * * * *

Two-thirds of the nation's helium is produced in **Dumas**.

* * * * *

Spring is the home base for the Goodyear blimp "America."

* * * * *

Westlaco took its name from the W.E. Stewart Land Company's initials, who promoted the town site in 1919.

* * * * *

The Woodlands Trail in **Jefferson** features a 99-foot yellow poplar, brought to Texas in 1887 from Georgia.

* * * * *

Kountze produces 5.5 million board feet of lumber yearly.

* * * * *

The Queen of Peace statue and the Oriental Gardens at Port Arthur are decorated with **700,000 lights** at Christmas time.

* * * * *

Lubbock claims to be the **Chrysanthemum Capital** of the World. Judge for yourself in late October.

* * * * *

Indianola was the site where two shiploads of **Arabian camels** landed for the experiment Jefferson Davis wanted to conduct using the camels for transportation and communications.

* * * * *

Women and children were once forbidden to be in **Cuero** after dark. Seems it got a bit rough around sundown.

* * * * *

Stanton was settled in 1881 by German Catholics. The town's original name was **Marienfeld,** or field of Mary.

* * * * *

Dalhart was first called **Twist.**

* * * * *

William Travis, Sam Houston, and David Burnet all practiced law in **Liberty**.

* * * * *

Vernon was first called **Eagle Flats** after the nesting eagles in the area.

* * * * *

The **LBJ Ranch,** home of the late President, is located in Stonewall.

* * * * *

Jefferson was the state's first city to use **artificial gas** for street lighting.

* * * * *

The city of **Crockett** was named for David Crockett. Legend says that he stopped here to camp by a spring that still flows, Davy Crockett Spring.

* * * * *

There are only **two towns** in Briscoe County.

* * * * *

El Paso is the largest U.S. city on the Mexican border. Just across the border is Juarez, Mexico's largest border city. Together these cities house a population of about 1.7 million people.

* * * * *

Harmony Hill Ghost Town is 18 miles northeast of Henderson. In 1850 it was an important trade center known as **Nip and Tuck**. Only a large cemetery is there today.

* * * * *

Lufkin is in the heart of the East Texas Piney Woods region.

* * * * *

The nation's two longest highways, U.S. 90 and U.S. 83, intersect at **Uvalde**.

* * * * *

Llano calls itself the "Deer Capital of Texas."

* * * * *

The city of **Alamo** was not named after the Alamo, but for Alamo Land and Sugar Co.

* * * * *

Coldspring was founded in 1847 as **Coonskin**.

* * * * *

Port Aransas is on **Mustang Island** and can be reached by the causeway or by the free 24-hour ferry service.

* * * * *

The city of **Ysleta** became part of Texas following a change in the Rio Grande's course...it was in Mexico! Ysleta is the oldest town in Texas.

* * * * *

Marble Falls is the location where, in the 1880s, quarrying began for the highly prized pink and red granite to construct the State Capitol. The quarrying has continued to this day, and the huge dome of granite has been affected very little. Visitors are not admitted in the quarry site, but you can view the operation from a roadside picnic area on R.M. 1431, north of Marble Falls.

* * * * *

Dumas is in the heart of our nation's largest grain sorghum producing area.

* * * * *

Fort Davis has been the county seat of Presidio and Jeff Davis counties.

* * * * *

Franklin was established as the town of **Morgan** in 1871.

* * * * *

Gail is the county seat of Borden County—and the **only town in Borden County**. There is a courthouse but no bank, doctor, or lawyer.

* * * * *

The town of **Taylorsville** is known as Decatur today.

* * * * *

Val Verde County consists of more than 30,000 square miles.

* * * * *

Del Rio calls itself the "Queen City of the Rio Grande."

* * * * *

Columbus calls itself "The City of Live Oaks."

* * * * *

Columbus was once the site of an Indian village called **Montezuma**.

* * * * *

Delta County is known as the "Vetch Capital of the World."

* * * * *

Corsicana was the first city in Texas to use **natural gas** for fuel and lighting.

* * * * *

Corsicana was the first city in the state to use crude oil for locomotive fuel.

* * * * *

Caldwell has been the seat of two counties. **Caldwell** is the seat of Burleson County, but before Burleson was organized in 1846, Caldwell was the Milam County seat.

* * * * *

Clarendon was established in 1878 by a Methodist minister, L. H. Carhart, as a "**sobriety settlement**." The town was known as "Saints Roost."

* * * * *

From the original **Red River County**, created in 1836 as one of the original Texas counties, all or part of 38 other counties were created.

* * * * *

Cleburne was first known as **Camp Henderson**. The name was changed in 1867.

* * * * *

Bandera was founded in 1852 as a cypress shingle camp, and in 1854 Bandera became the site of a Mormon colony.

* * * * *

Boerne was formally established in 1851 by German settlers. The town grew from a village called Tusculum established in 1849.

* * * * *

Alice was first called Kleberg. Later the town was named after the daughter of one of the founders of the King Ranch.

* * * * *

Athens was either named after the capital of Greece or Athens, Georgia. Local residents cannot agree.

* * * * *

Atlanta was named for Atlanta, Georgia.

* * * * *

Runnels County is cut by the **Colorado River**.

* * * * *

Ballinger was established in 1886 as Hutchins City.

* * * * *

Trappers and explorers established **Beaumont** as a trading post in the early 1800s. In 1901 the world's first oil gusher, Spindletop, put Beaumont on the map.

* * * * *

Big Sandy was the first settlement of the woodlands area. The settlement originated from Mexican land grants of 1835 and was named for nearby Sandy Creek.

* * * * *

The settlement that became **Buffalo Gap** was located at the site of a natural pass in the Callahan Divide that buffalo traveled. Buffalo Gap was also located on the Dodge Cattle Trail.

* * * * *

Round Rock was established in 1850 and was named for a large round rock in the bed of Brushy Creek. The rock was used by travelers as a landmark and was the point they used to cross the creek.

* * * * *

Taylor was originally named Taylorsville.

* * * * *

Corpus Christi's slogan is "Sparkling City by the Sea."

* * * * *

Deckman was the original name of **Grand Prairie**. The name was changed in 1873.

* * * * *

Irving was established in 1902 as a site for a watermelon farm owned by J.O. Schulze and Otis Brown. In 1906 these men donated farmland to the railroad, which is much of present-day Irving.

* * * * *

Mesquite was established in 1872 and named for nearby Mesquite Creek.

* * * * *

Plano was first settled in 1845 and named Fillmore after Millard Fillmore. The name was changed to Plano in 1851.

* * * * *

The settlement known as Breckenridge before the Civil War is known as **Richardson** today.

* * * * *

Anthony, incorporated in 1952, is a two-state city. The town is located on the border between Texas and New Mexico.

* * * * *

Magoffinsville community later became **El Paso**.

* * * * *

El Paso is "V" shaped.

* * * * *

Deer Park, founded in 1892 by Simeon West, was named for the abundance of deer in the area.

* * * * *

The name **Pasadena** is Spanish for Land of Flowers.

* * * * *

Texas City was originally called Shoal Point.

* * * * *

Bastrop is one of Texas' oldest settlements, and it was first called Mina.

* * * * *

The county jail in **Hemphill** has only four cells—and a gallows that has been there for more than 80 years.

* * * * *

Hondo is Spanish for deep. The city took its name from Hondo Creek.

* * * * *

Huntsville is the headquarters of the Texas Department of Criminal Justice, Institutional Division.

* * * * *

Huntsville was once the center of culture and known as the "**Athens of Texas.**"

* * * * *

The village of **Lajitas** came into existence in 1915 when an army post was set up to protect the Big Bend area from the Mexican bandit Pancho Villa. **Lajitas** is Spanish for flagstones.

* * * * *

Longview was named in 1870 by surveyors for the railroad who were impressed with the long-distance view from the town.

* * * * *

McLean was a former site of a World War II German prisoner of war camp.

* * * * *

Meridian was established on July 4, 1854 as the seat of the newly created Bosque County. The town was named for its location on the 100th meridian.

Chapter 3

* * * * *

Midland was named for its location—halfway between El Paso and Fort Worth.

* * * * *

In 1852, settlers from Perry, Illinois established the town of Perry, Texas. Perry was renamed **Moody** in 1881 in honor of Col. W. L. Moody.

* * * * *

Pecos was the site of a cowboy contest in 1883 that probably started our present-day rodeo contests. Because of this, Pecos claims the title of "Home of the World's First Rodeo."

* * * * *

Pleasanton claims the title "Birthplace of the Cowboy" since, before the town was established in 1858, there were Spaniards, Mexicans, and Americans ranching in the area. Pleasanton was the first to claim the title. Several cities in the area could have, but for whatever reason did not. The exact location is not known, only the general area.

* * * * *

The "Strawberry Capital of Texas" is **Poteet**.

* * * * *

Established in 1835 as Jones Post Office, **Round Top** is one of the smallest incorporated cities in Texas—population 81.

* * * * *

When **Rusk** was chosen as the county seat of Cherokee County in 1846, only one family was living there.

* * * * *

Salado was named for the Salado Creek. Salado means salty.

* * * * *

San Augustine is known as "The Cradle of Texas."

* * * * *

The Immaculate Conception Catholic Church in **Panna Maria** has a cross on the building that was brought from Poland by the original settlers in the 1850s.

* * * * *

The **first Spanish mission** in East Texas was San Francisco de los Tejas, built in 1690 and moved to San Antonio in 1731. A com-

58

memorative structure of the mission is located in Mission Tejas State Historic Park southwest of Weches.

* * * * *

The first Spanish mission in Texas was established in 1682 near **El Paso**, called Corpus Christi de la Isleta.

* * * * *

Fort Martin Scott, outside Fredericksburg, was the first federal fort established in Texas. When the fort was established in 1848, they found that the German settlers had already drawn up a treaty with the Comanche Indians, and the treaty was never broken by either side.

* * * * *

The **Grace Episcopal Church** in Cuero is a century old, and its steeple is sheathed in copper.

* * * * *

Galveston had the first Texas Roman Catholic convent.

* * * * *

St. Mary's Cathedral built in 1848, in Galveston, was the first Catholic cathedral in Texas.

* * * * *

Fort Hood in Killeen is the only two-division army post in the nation.

* * * * *

The "Birthplace of Anglo-American Settlement in Texas" is San Felipe—actually it is **San Felipe de Austin,** named for Stephen F. Austin.

* * * * *

Texas puts oil wells everywhere—don't believe me? In **Lake Arrowhead** you can see more than a dozen steel derricks over oil wells in the lake itself.

* * * * *

When oil was discovered in **Ranger** in 1917, the population grew from 1,000 to 30,000 people in one year.

* * * * *

The discovery of oil on land owned by the **University of Texas**, in 1923, made it one of the richest schools in the nation. The Santa Rita No. 1 was an 8,525-foot well that was productive from the time of the gusher on May 28, 1923 until 1990. A historical marker is outside the fenced-off area where you can still see some of the original equipment used during the 1923 gusher.

* * * * *

Nearly a **million barrels** of crude oil are refined in the Port Arthur area daily.

* * * * *

William Barrett Travis, hero and commander at the Alamo, was born August 9, 1809, in South Carolina.

* * * * *

The **first marriage** sanctioned under the laws of the Republic of Texas was held October 12, 1836, between George Webb Slaughter and Sarah Mason.

* * * * *

December 22, 1912 is the birthday of **Claudia Alta Taylor**—Mrs. LBJ—born in Karnack.

* * * * *

Alvin is known as the City of Beautiful Trees. About 1907, the Civic Club sponsored a tree planting campaign that added about 400 live oak trees to Alvin, and in 1924 the mayor urged everyone to plant at least one tree in their yards. Those trees are grown now and Alvin is still sponsoring tree planting campaigns.

* * * * *

Did you know that the median age of folks in **Abilene** is 29.7 years, according to the 1990 census.

* * * * *

The area that is now **Abilene State Park** in Buffalo Gap was once a resting place for the Comanche Indians. The park covers over 600 acres with more than 4000 native pecan trees.

* * * * *

Andrews County has only one incorporated city, **Andrews**. By the way, there are 1500 square miles in Andrews County!

* * * * *

New York, Texas, is 90 miles southeast of Dallas with a population of 12. This little town has one of the most stolen road signs in the state of Texas!

* * * * *

The first and only attempted bank robbery in the city of **Baird** took place on September 25, 1936. The robber was forced to leave before any money was taken, and he was apprehended 35 minutes later and locked in jail!

* * * * *

The population of **Beaumont** was around 8500 in 1901, but within 30 days of the Spindletop oil discovery on January 10, the population exploded to 30,000.

* * * * *

The U.S. Senate proclaimed **Beaumont**, Texas, as the "Pro-Football Capital of the World" since so many men from Beaumont play professional football.

* * * * *

In 1839 voters had to choose between Bastrop or Waterloo for the site of the new state capital. **Waterloo** won and changed its name to Austin. Waterloo, Texas, hummm . . . .

* * * * *

The Carnegie Library building in **Ballinger** is one of 34 library buildings funded by the philanthropist Andrew Carnegie, and it is one of only four of those buildings still being used as a public library. The library was completed in 1911.

* * * * *

In 1987 the population of **Bee County** was 28,321 with a per capita income of $9,766.00.

* * * * *

Boerne is known as the Key to the Hills.

* * * * *

Charles Harris was the only man in **Montague County** to be legally hanged for killing his brother.

* * * * *

Did you know that **Forestburg** does not have a cemetery in town? The town sits on top of several rock layers, and so the people had to go outside of town to find a sandy area to establish a cemetery.

* * * * *

The **Bluebonnet Capital** of Texas is Burnet—acclaimed by the Texas Legislature.

* * * * *

Bridge City is surrounded on three sides by waterways—the Neches River, Sabine Lake, and Cow Bayou.

* * * * *

Brady is the geographical center of Texas.

* * * * *

The city of **Breckenridge** started out as Breckinridge, but around the 1880s the name was misspelled, and the new spelling took hold and remains today.

* * * * *

Bandera is the only incorporated city in Bandera County, population 877 in 1992.

* * * * *

Columbus claims to be Texas' oldest permanently established Anglo-American settlement. Columbus was laid out in August 1823 and except for a few weeks in 1836, during the Revolution, has been in continuous occupancy. Washington-on-the-Brazos was laid out in 1824, and the first building was not built until 1830. San Felipe, another contender for the title, was abandoned by 1843.

* * * * *

Three rear-admirals of World War II came from **Calvert**: Admiral Marion Robertson, Admiral Spencer Lewis, and Admiral Ernest Pace. All were graduates of the U.S. Naval Academy at Annapolis.

* * * * *

Sam Houston proposed **Wheelock** as the capital of Texas—he had a horse ranch there and liked to visit.

* * * * *

She was born Rosa Lee Moore Hall, a native of Pin Oak, between Hearne and Wheelock. Rosa Lee moved to Oklahoma City where she went to work for the Quaker Oats Co. Her face was on millions of packages of pancake mix, flour, and syrup until 1989. Rosa Lee died and was buried in Pin Oak in 1967. Rosa Lee was "**Aunt Jemima**."

* * * * *

There is a community in Shelby County, southeast of Center, called **Choice**. In 1904 the town was founded but had no name, and the people had to pick a name to be submitted to the post office. After a lot of discussion, they had to make a choice, so Choice is what was put on the application.

* * * * *

Caldwell is the Kolache Capital of Texas.

* * * * *

Childress County was created in 1876 and named for an attorney, George C. Childress, a member of the 1836 convention and co-author of the Texas Declaration of Independence.

* * * * *

Jim Reeves was born August 20, 1923 at his family home in **DeBerry** in Panola County. He graduated from Carthage High School in 1942. After signing to play for the St. Louis Cardinals, Reeves injured his leg and ended his baseball career. In 1946 he started singing country music, and three of his records sold over a million copies. After a plane crash killed him on July 31, 1964, near Nashville, Tennessee, his body was returned to Carthage. A life-size statue of Reeves stands over the grave. In 1967 his collie, Cheyenne, was buried ten paces behind him.

* * * * *

Panola is an Indian word meaning cotton.

* * * * *

Tex Ritter, member of the Country Music Hall of Fame, was born in Panola County.

* * * * *

Montell is in northern Uvalde County and has a population of 14.

* * * * *

The annual meetings of the Texas Greyhound Association are held in **Cameron**.

* * * * *

Cleveland was incorporated in 1935, but no city taxes were collected until 1947.

* * * * *

Castroville is "The Little Alsace of Texas." Henry Castro, of France, brought settlers to the area, mostly from the French province of Alsace. Henry Castro was second only to Stephen F. Austin in the number of settlers he brought into Texas. He was born in France, was of Portuguese descent, was Jewish in belief, an American citizen, and a Texas empressario. During a trip to Monterrey, Mexico, he died and was buried in an unmarked grave.

* * * * *

Castroville has **two town squares**: Houston Square in the center of Old Castroville, and September Square, named to commemorate the fact that settlers first arrived on September 4, 1844.

* * * * *

The **Santa Anna Mountain** contains vast amounts of silica sand, or glass sand. Santa Anna ceramic tile is famous for its quality.

* * * * *

Cedar Hill is the **highest point** between the Rio Grande and the Red River. The pioneers liked this location because they felt like they could see the Indians coming and have time to get ready for any attacks.

* * * * *

In 1846 **Cedar Hill** became the Dallas County seat, and all the county records were moved until a permanent site could be chosen. Two elections later, Dallas was named the county seat.

* * * * *

In 1954 the first communication tower was erected in Cedar Hill. **Cedar Hill** became home to many giant towers and soon was known as the "Tower City of the Southwest."

* * * * *

The city of **Cisco** started as the small community of Red Gap in 1881.

* * * * *

Bronte was named for the English novelist Charlotte Bronte.

* * * * *

Haskell was previously known as Willow Pond Springs, and later it was called Rice Springs. The present name was chosen in 1885 when the post office was established.

* * * * *

Cut and Shoot, located five miles east of Conroe, was incorporated on April 5, 1969, with a population of 300. The population has grown to around 900 and does not have a city tax.

* * * * *

The little town of **Splendora**, in Montgomery County, began as Cox's Switch, but the name was changed because of the splendor of the area.

* * * * *

Outside the Kaufman County Courthouse, at the county seat of Kaufman. Kaufman is about 40-50 miles southeast of Dallas.

The first automobile accident is remembered in the town of Forney, east of Dallas. The sign is displayed in the city park, just off Highway 80 East.

La Salle County has over 1 million acres.

* * * * *

Did you know the **Corpus Christi** seawall was designed by Guzon Borglum? Who is that? He was the sculptor of Mt. Rushmore!

* * * * *

Port Aransas is the Deep Sea Fishing Capital of Texas.

* * * * *

President Franklin Roosevelt came to **Port Aransas** to fish for tarpon quite frequently and helped put the area on the map as a great place to come for deep sea fishing.

* * * * *

In 1818 **Dr. James Long**, his wife, and one child came to Texas with approximately 300 troops to free Texas from Spain. Dr. Long set up his operations at Port Bolivar in 1820. When the troops and Dr. Long moved on toward Mexico, they left Mrs. Long at the fort. On December 21, 1821, she gave birth to a daughter, Mary, believed to be the first white child born in Texas. Mrs. Long left the fort in July of 1822 after word came that her husband had been killed. She ran a boarding house for many years and died in 1880 in Richmond, Texas. Jane Long is often referred to as "The Mother of Texas."

* * * * *

The **Bolivar Peninsula** first received electricity in 1948, telephones in 1957, and the first piped water system was built in 1969. This is not surprising since the peninsula is accessible only by state highway ferries or by one state highway on the eastern end.

* * * * *

The **Golden Crescent** area is made up of seven counties—Calhoun, DeWitt, Goliad, Gonzales, Jackson, Lavaca, and Victoria.

* * * * *

Which is the "Cleanest Little City in Texas"? **Shiner**.

* * * * *

The destruction of **Indianola** by storms influenced the growth of Victoria. Indianola, a ghost town today with only memorials to remember the city, was hit by a hurricane in 1875, another in 1880, and a third storm in 1886. The people couldn't keep up with the destruction and rebuilding. Many of the houses from Indianola that could be salvaged were dismantled and moved to Victoria and rebuilt.

* * * * *

Ogletree Gap Valley, about 2 miles west of Copperas Cove, is the original town site. The Tonkawa Indians had inhabited the valley area, and some of the rock fences, built by the Indians to keep their cattle, can still be found on the hills around the valley.

* * * * *

Waxahachie is becoming one of the most acclaimed movie sets in the nation—the whole town. Hollywood loves the historic homes and the people who are willing to put up with the inconvenience of almost shutting down the town for filming. Films such as *Places In The Heart, Tender Mercies,* and *The Trip To Bountiful* have been filmed in Waxahachie.

* * * * *

Judge Thomas J. Devine was born in Nova Scotia and came to Texas in 1843. He was a judge in the San Antonio area that tried Union sympathizers during the Civil War and went to Mexico at war's end to continue the fight from there. What makes Judge Devine special is that he was twice indicted for treason. He is the only Southerner to have that distinction, with the exception of President Jefferson Davis. Judge Devine was pardoned in June of 1867 by President Andrew Johnson, and the town of Devine was named for him in 1881.

* * * * *

Anson Jones was elected president of Texas in September 1844— and he didn't even make a campaign speech. He was the last president of Texas, serving until February 19, 1846, at which time Texas became a state. Anson Jones took his life with a gun on January 9, 1858, in Houston. The city of Anson is the county seat of Jones County—both were named for Anson Jones.

* * * * *

Born in Denison, Texas, on October 14, 1890, **Dwight David Eisenhower's** application to West Point mistakenly listed Tyler, Texas, as his birthplace. The family moved to Kansas after his birth. Once General Eisenhower became very popular during World War II, Jennie Jackson, who was principal of Lamar Elementary School, remembered a family of Eisenhowers that lived in Denison and a baby named David. After Jennie Jackson contacted Mrs. Eisenhower, she did confirm the fact that Dwight was born in Denison.

Mrs. Eisenhower had reversed the President's name, from David Dwight to Dwight David, when he got older, to make it easier to talk to either Dwight or his father, David. His birthplace and the surrounding city block is now a state historical park. One point of interest, the only authentic Eisenhower possession in the house is the quilt in the bedroom where President Eisenhower was born.

* * * * *

Did you know that Dwight D. Eisenhower and Thomas V. Munson both received the French Legion of Honor, and both were from **Denison**? Mr. Munson was the second American to receive the award—for saving the grape industry in France. Eisenhower was the third American to receive the honor. Who was the first? Thomas Edison.

* * * * *

The Goose Hunting Capital of the World is **Eagle Lake**.

* * * * *

El Sal Del Rey, or Salt of the King, is a salt lake discovered in 1687 by Spanish explorers and claimed for the King of Spain, Charles IV. **Salt Lake** is 22 miles north of Edinburg, and for more than 200 years the lake was a source of pure rock salt.

* * * * *

In early days, **Hempstead** was known as "Six Shooter Junction;" now it is often referred to as the "Watermelon Capital of the World."

* * * * *

The Pompeiian villa in **Port Arthur** was built for Issac Ellwood, the "Barbed Wire King." The vacation home is pink.

* * * * *

Nederland was founded by Dutch immigrants in 1898. Nederland was also the home of Tex Ritter. A replica of a Dutch windmill stands today as a museum honoring the Dutch heritage of the area, and it also contains mementos of Tex Ritter.

* * * * *

Paris is named for Paris, France, and claims to be the "Second Largest Paris in the World."

* * * * *

Originally known as "**Macaroni Station**," the town of **Edna** started as a train station which housed food and supplies for the Italian workers for the New York, Texas, and Mexico Railway (NYTM).

Count Joseph Telferner, an Italian nobleman and financier, sponsored the rail lines in the southwest Texas area. Edna incorporated in May of 1899 and unincorporated in September of 1899. The people did not like the rules that came with incorporation. It was not until 1929 that Edna once again incorporated.

* * * * *

Elgin has the title "The Brick Capital of the Southwest" because of three brick manufacturing companies in the area.

* * * * *

Terlingua is a ghost town west of Big Bend National Park. Nothing is left of the town but the remains of the quicksilver mines and the old cemetery.

* * * * *

Forney was founded as **Brooklyn** in the 1860s and renamed in 1873 after Col. John W. Forney, publisher and railroad executive.

* * * * *

The Texas State Legislature designated **Forney** "Antique Capital of Texas" in 1987.

* * * * *

The "Peanut Capital of Texas" is **Floresville,** and the Peanut Festival is the second Friday and Saturday of October each year.

* * * * *

The small town of **Luckenbach** was purchased in 1970 by the late Hondo Crouch. The town continues to be privately owned.

* * * * *

Admiral Nimitz was born in Fredericksburg. His grandparents were some of the first settlers in the area and were the owners of the Nimitz Hotel.

* * * * *

Falfurrias is a Lipan Indian word meaning "The Land of Heart's Delight." A story tells of a Lipan Indian brave looking over the area and saying falfurrias, and the name remained. A wildflower found in the area is also called falfurrias.

* * * * *

Don Pedrito was a faith healer born in Jalisco, Mexico, who came to the Falfurrias area, the Los Olmos Ranch, in 1881. For 25 years he helped thousands of people, never charging for his services, and anything given to him went to charity. There is a Texas Historical

Marker honoring Don Pedrito, and his shrine is still visited by thousands of people each year.

* * * * *

The World's Richest Acre is in downtown **Kilgore**. Half a city block contained 24 wells that were drilled producing 2.5 million barrels of oil. Ten restored derricks stand on the historic acre.

* * * * *

Fredericksburg is well known for its "Sunday Houses." These were small structures that the farmers and ranchers built so they would have a place to stay when they came into town for supplies and to go to church on Sunday. Most of the farmers and ranchers lived too far to make the trip and take care of their business in town in one day, so the "Sunday Houses" provided a home away from home. Several of these houses remain today.

* * * * *

Gainesville was first settled by "49ers" who had started west on the California Trail, passed through this area, and decided to stay. This is where California Street gets its name.

* * * * *

Samuel May Williams was known as the "Father of the Texas Navy."

* * * * *

Pirate **Jean LaFitte** lived on Galveston Island from 1817 to 1821. After an attack on a U.S. ship, LaFitte and his men were forced to leave the island.

* * * * *

Did you know that the Williamson County Courthouse has a **copper dome**?

* * * * *

In 1910, 6000 pecan trees were set out on a 385-acre tract of land which later became the city of **Groves**. Several years later this tract of land was sold to a real estate syndicate, and Mr. Asa B. Groves was sent to represent the company as the land was developed into a residential subdivision. Groves is named for Mr. Groves, however, the groves of pecan trees strengthened the name of the community. The Groves Pecan Festival started in 1968, and the House of Representatives, of the 72nd Legislature, declared the annual festival at the end of September to be the official Texas Pecan Festival.

* * * * *

Elizabeth Crockett, Davy Crockett's second wife, moved to Granbury in 1856 to claim the land that Texas gave to the heirs of the men who died at the Alamo—1280 acres.

* * * * *

Grapevine was so called in 1854 because of its location on Grape Vine Prairie, and it was near Grape Vine Springs. The area was named for the mustang grapes that were abundant in the area. It was only fitting that the town be called Grapevine.

* * * * *

Henderson King Yoakum, historian and lawyer, is best known as the author of Texas' first history book, published in 1855.

* * * * *

Dr. Pleasant W. Kittrell was Sam Houston's doctor at the time of his death.

* * * * *

Hitchock was the home of the U.S. Naval Air Station, called the Blimp Base, during World War II in 1942 and 1943.

* * * * *

Honey Grove sits on an imaginary dividing line between sandy soil to the north of town and black clay soil to the south.

* * * * *

The first settler of Honey Grove was **Samuel Erwin**. David Crockett had passed through and camped in the area just west of where town square is today. He wrote letters back to his home in Tennessee about this area and the abundance of honey in the hollow trees. Mr. Erwin was one of Crockett's friends and came to settle in the "honey grove" in 1842.

* * * * *

Naval Station Ingleside, located at Ingleside, is the new Mine Warfare Command Center for the U.S. Navy, opened in June of 1992—homeport for approximately 25 ships in the next five years. The first ship at the facility was the U.S.S. *Scout*—the first Navy ship to be homeported in Texas since World War II.

* * * * *

Jacksboro was named Mesquiteville from 1856 to 1858 because of the many large mesquite trees in the area. Jacksboro was first known as Lost Creek.

Chapter 3

* * * * *

The town of **Kermit** was named after Theodore Roosevelt's son. The town started out in 1910 with three houses, a four-room hotel, and a courthouse.

* * * * *

Anahuac is "Alligator Capital of Texas" as recognized by the Legislature in May of 1989—the first year of the Gatorfest. **Anahuac** has more alligators than it has people!

* * * * *

Van Cliburn, international concert pianist, is from Kilgore.

* * * * *

Laredo was founded in May 1755 by Don Tomas Sanchez, an officer of the Royal Army of Spain. Laredo claims to be one of the oldest cities in the country and has had seven flags flown over it—Spain, Mexico, Republic of Texas, Confederacy, United States, France, and the Republic of the Rio Grande.

* * * * *

Mansfield started out as Mansfeild. Two partners, Julian Feild and Ralph S. Man, established a grist mill and the settlement that grew up around the mill was called Mansfeild. After several misspellings over the years, the more conventional spelling of Mansfield was finally accepted.

* * * * *

Even though Bob Wills wasn't born in **Turkey,** he grew up there.

* * * * *

Merkel was once known as the city of windmills.

* * * * *

While drilling for water in 1893, **Marlin** citizens got a steaming geyser of mineral water that shot in the air 50 feet! Marlin is the location for several resorts specializing in naturally heated mineral baths.

* * * * *

Mr. Shary is called the **"Father of Valley Citrus,"** since he was the first person to grow citrus fruit commercially in the Rio Grande Valley. He is credited with the development of the citrus industry in Texas.

* * * * *

McAllen claims the title "Square Dance Capital of the World." It is possible to dance every hour of the day and into the night, any day of the week, in McAllen and the neighboring towns—there is always a dance going on. McAllen also hosts the Annual Texas Square Dance Jamboree.

* * * * *

In January 1929, **Lake Lovenskiold Reservoir** was created with the construction of La Fruita Dam across the Nueces River. In November of that same year, 1929, the dam was washed out. In 1935 the dam was rebuilt and the lake was renamed Lake Corpus Christi.

* * * * *

Cochran County was one of the original 23 counties created by the Republic of Texas. Cochran was not settled at the time that it was created. In fact, the 1890 census shows no residents listed. It was almost fifty years after its creation that the county was organized. By the way, the 1920 population count showed 67 people in Cochran County.

* * * * *

Miami was named for an Indian maid in 1887—supposed to be Minnie Ha Ha's twin sister. Miami comes from an Indian word meaning "sweetheart," and it is known as the "Sweetheart of the Plains."

* * * * *

The city of **Mineola** was designated in 1991 by the Legislature as the City of Festivals.

* * * * *

The **Mount Pleasant** name comes from the Caddo Indians. Mounds in and near the original town site were built by a prehistoric race, according to Caddo Indian legend. The Indians liked to camp near the red mineral springs, and the great mound became famous among the Caddos who called it Pleasant Mound. Early settlers continued the name of Pleasant Mound for a time, and then later changed it to Mount Pleasant.

* * * * *

There are **three Bostons** in Texas, all in the same area. Old Boston was the county seat of Bowie County until fire destroyed the town in the 1870s and the seat was moved to Boston, the geographic center of Bowie County. The new courthouse is located in New Boston even though the county seat is in Boston. Old Boston, Boston, and New Boston are within four miles of each other.

* * * * *

Texas' **first millionaire** was Frost Thorn, born in Glen Cove, New York—New York?!

* * * * *

During the late 1890s, **Naples** was a pretty rough town, and women and children were not on the streets after sundown.

* * * * *

Orange was first known as Green's Bluff. It was also known as Huntly, Lower Town of Jefferson, Madison, and then as Orange, because of the native orange groves—or was it because the color orange was the mayor's favorite color? There is still discussion on this point.

* * * * *

Don't you just love the welcome sign as you go into **Dumas**—"Welcome to Dumas…13,000 friendly folks and a few old soreheads."

* * * * *

One story tells that **Odessa** was named by the Russian men working on the railroad line. The area reminded them of Odessa, Russia, with the wide, flat prairies.

* * * * *

Did you know that after **President Bush** graduated from Yale in 1948, he and Barbara and son George moved to Odessa—their first Texas home.

* * * * *

Luling has 184 oil wells in the city limits and more in the surrounding area. Since the people of Luling have a wonderful sense of humor and are extremely creative, some of the local people "dressed up" their pump jacks and made mobile art out of them! Butterflies, tigers, cartoon characters, Santa Claus—wonderful moving sculptures! The Chamber of Commerce even commissioned a local sign artist to create moving sculptures. Sounds like a fun place to live!

* * * * *

Located in Frio County about 17 miles from Pearsall and a ghost town now, **Frio Town** has only a few memories left—the old courthouse, the jail, and a few brick chimneys. Famous characters once graced the jail; the James Brothers and Sam Bass were a few. How do we know since the town is no more? They wrote their names on the walls of their jail cells—yes, the signatures are still there.

* * * * *

Country singer **George Strait** was born in a hospital in Poteet, but he came home to Pearsall.

* * * * *

Bigfoot was founded in 1865 and named for "Bigfoot" Wallace— actually he was William Alexander Anderson Wallace. Wallace was an Indian fighter, mail carrier, and a Texas Ranger. He wasn't nicknamed "Bigfoot" because he had big feet; he was named that after he killed an Indian with big feet!

* * * * *

The Scientific Balloon Facility of the National Center for Atmospheric Research was established in 1961 in Boulder, Colorado. The facility was moved to Palestine in 1963, and in 1973 it was designated the **National Scientific Balloon Facility**. In 1982 sponsorship of the facility was transferred to NASA. In its 25 years of service, over 1700 balloons have been launched for numerous universities, research, and foreign groups. The services the facility provides are inflation, launching of the balloons, tracking and recovery of the payload, and telecommand and data retrieval. The design of the systems and research into balloon materials, power systems, and recovery systems make this facility recognized internationally as one of the most advanced of its type in the world.

* * * * *

In its early years, **Harlingen** was commonly called "Six Shooter Junction" by the railroad conductors pulling into town.

* * * * *

Port Isabel was known as Point Isabel until 1930.

* * * * *

Did you know that **Houston** was jealous of the port in Galveston but couldn't compete—that is until Houston dredged a 45-mile channel from the Gulf of Mexico!

* * * * *

Pasadena was named after Pasadena, California.

* * * * *

Pilot Point was named for a high point that was used as a marker for travelers going west. The town was laid out on Christmas Day in 1854.

* * * * *

Val Keene Whitacre is credited with finding the first **Plainview point** in 1941. The area the point was found in has yielded some very important archeological finds, including bones of an extinct bison twice the size of today's variety.

* * * * *

With beginnings as a fishing settlement, **Port O'Connor** was originally called Alligator Head.

* * * * *

The town of **Post** was founded in 1907 by Charles Post of breakfast cereal fame and fortune. Mr. Post bought 300,000 acres in 1903 and financed and oversaw the building of the town, without regard to profit. Settlers were offered homes that cost $1500 and up. The houses required a $30 down payment and $15 per month payments with no interest charged. When water became scarce, Mr. Post conducted experiments with dynamite to make it rain—22 times he used the dynamite and 8 times it rained. Even after his death in 1914, his daughter Marjorie came to the town's rescue with loans to the farmers during a long drought in 1919.

* * * * *

Plano is the sister city to Ivanovo, Russia, 200 miles from Moscow.

* * * * *

The town of **Round Top** was first known as Townsend because of five families of that name living in the area. Later it was known as Jones Post Office. Mr. Soergel built an octagonal structure that became a landmark in the 1840s. The house was nicknamed "the house with the round top," and the town's name gradually changed around this point of interest.

* * * * *

Rosebud was named for the beautiful roses in Mrs. Mullins' yard, which she brought with her from her home in Washington County. J.R. Killgore, owner of the *Rosebud News*, started the "A Rosebush in Every Yard" movement and gave away cuttings to anyone who did not have a rose bush. Even though Mr. Killgore has passed away, his wife and sons, who run the paper, still give away rose bush cuttings. Ripley's "Believe It Or Not" published the fact that "There's a rose bush in every yard in Rosebud, Texas." And what is the town motto? "Everything's Rosy In Rosebud," of course.

* * * * *

There is no official record of when **Rowlett** was established. Until 1836 it was referred to as the German Settlement. Daniel Owen Rowlett came to Texas and was given a land grant which included a creek. Later the creek was referred to as Rowlett's Creek, and the community that grew up around the creek assumed the name of the creek.

* * * * *

You can only get to **Matagorda Island** by boat. The island is the only barrier island in public ownership, owned by the state of Texas and U.S. Fish and Wildlife service.

* * * * *

The **Presidio La Bahia** in Goliad is the only completely restored Spanish colonial Presidio in the western hemisphere. Did you know the Presidio was the only North American fort to witness six national wars for independence?

* * * * *

T.J. Rusk **never actually ran for office**, but when he was drafted for an official position, he was never defeated. He was supposed to have held more high official positions than any other man during the days of the Texas Republic.

* * * * *

Los Ebanos Ferry, located west of Mission, the only remaining **hand-drawn ferry** across the Rio Grande River in the U.S., has had its anchor cable tied to an ebony tree for the last 50 years. The ebony tree is estimated to be 250 years old. The area where the ferry crosses was once known as "Smugglers Crossing"—liquor would be transported in the night during prohibition. There are also stories of ghost sightings at the ferry. The ferry, connecting the U.S. with Diaz Ordaz, Mexico, will soon be replaced with a bridge that is under construction.

* * * * *

San Angelo started out as Saint Angela in 1870. Bart DeWitt named the town after his deceased wife, Angela de la Garza. Later the name was corrupted to San Angela and in 1883 postal authorities changed the name to San Angelo, since San was masculine and Angela was feminine.

* * * * *

San Augustine is known as the Cradle of Texas. It had its beginning in 1716 when the Mission Nuestra Senora de los Delores de los Ais was established for the Ais Indians. San Augustine claims to be the oldest Anglo town in Texas.

* * * * *

San Marcos is on a buffalo trail that became the Camino Real.

* * * * *

Did you know that **Frances Cox Henderson**, the wife of the first governor of Texas, spoke 18 languages fluently and 7 more languages rather well. She was supposed to have been able to read the Bible in 30 languages.

* * * * *

Did you know that **Seguin** was declared the county seat of Guadalupe County before the county was created? Seguin was declared the Seat of Justice in the County of Guadalupe, by the Legislature on March 24, 1846. It wasn't until six days later, on March 30, 1846, that the same Legislature created Guadalupe County from parts of Bexar and Gonzales counties.

* * * * *

Buffalo hunting was a very important trade in the first days of Snyder and Scurry County. Pete Snyder, a Dutch trader, established a trading post which the town of **Snyder** grew around. In fact, a buffalo hide house once stood where the Scurry County courthouse is now.

* * * * *

Stratford is called the "**Tip Top Town in Texas**" since it is the northernmost town located at the top of Texas. The town was named after the birthplace of General Robert E. Lee.

* * * * *

The town of **Stratford** claims the title "The Pheasant Capital of Texas." Pheasant season begins the second weekend in December and continues for two weeks.

* * * * *

When the water level of Falcon Dam is down, several buildings can be seen. One of the buildings is the **Mission Ampuero** at Revilla founded in 1750. The town of Viejo Guerrero was completely submerged by the waters of the dam in 1953. Viejo means old.

* * * * *

Cumby, at one time, was called Black Jack Grove because of the very large blackjack oak trees that were all over the area.

* * * * *

Did you know there was a **Bucksnort** in Hopkins County? The town is now extinct.

* * * * *

The name of **Sulphur Springs** pretty well tells the story of how the town got its name. The area was a good camping area for travelers with many springs for drinking water. Some of the springs were strong with sulphur, thus the name of the town, Sulphur Springs.

* * * * *

The sign greeting you into **Stanton** reads: "Welcome to Stanton, Home of 3000 friendly people and a few old soreheads."

* * * * *

The original **Sugar Land** was a company town built around the Imperial Sugar Company. The town consisted of rice farms and sugar cane fields. The company began around 1843 when the cane was cut and granulated on the Oakland Plantation. Imperial Sugar Company is the oldest business in Texas operating at its original location. In 1988 Imperial merged with Holly to form the third largest sugar company in the nation, now called Imperial Holly Sugar Company. Holly is a sugar beet processor, and the merger aided both companies against fluctuations in the market.

* * * * *

President Johnson was the first recipient of the National Education Association's annual Friend of Education Award in 1972. In 1965 Johnson signed into law the Elementary and Secondary Education Bill, and during his administration more than 60 pieces of educational legislation were passed.

* * * * *

Temple was called by many nicknames in its early days, names such as Mudville, Tanglefoot, and Ratsville.

* * * * *

Temple is known as the "Wildflower Capital of Texas."

* * * * *

Did you know that **Temple** is within three hours driving time of 80% of the state? I haven't tried it yet, but that is what they tell me.

* * * * *

Did you know that there is a **Utopia**, Texas? The town is close to the Uvalde area and was given its name because of the ideal climate. Utopia's original name was Waresville and was the first nonmilitary colony in Uvalde County.

* * * * *

Dale Evans is from Uvalde.

* * * * *

Uvalde County claims the title "country of eleven hundred springs" since it has more clear running streams than any other county in Texas. You can see the pebbles on the river bed bottoms under six feet of water. This is one reason that **Garner State Park** is a favorite spot and the most attended state park in Texas.

* * * * *

The Colony is a town built by a housing company, Fox & Jacobs Company. They purchased the land in 1969, planned and developed the area, and started building houses in 1974. By 1977 there were over 5000 residents, and the city was incorporated as "The Colony," getting its name from the Peters Colony. All but a few homes in the area have been built by Fox & Jacobs. Guess what the first business in The Colony was—a real estate company! What else! A small corner grocery was second!

* * * * *

Upshur County is almost 50% wooded and timber is one of the top income producing crops of the county.

* * * * *

The youngest man elected to the office of governor was **Dan Moody,** from Taylor; he was 33. Moody served from 1927 to 1931. Before serving as governor, District Attorney Moody went after the Ku Klux Klan, breaking their strength, and his energy resulted in his election to the office of attorney general. His continuous fight against corruption later led to his election as governor.

* * * * *

Texarkana is the combination of three state names—Texas, Arkansas, and Louisiana. Located on the Texas-Arkansas state line, the town is 25 miles north of the Louisiana border.

* * * * *

Along the **Texas Mountain Trail**, around Van Horn, 90 mountain peaks along the trail rise more than a mile high. Designated the "Crossroads of the Texas Mountain Trail" by the state, Van Horn is centrally located among the mountains of West Texas. The Texas Mountain Trail leads out of Van Horn in every direction.

* * * * *

Crockett County is named after **David Crockett**, but he never visited the area before his death at the Alamo. In 1939 a statue of Crockett was placed in the Ozona town square, to watch over the county that bears his name.

* * * * *

Port Arthur is known as the **Cajun Capital** of Southeast Texas.

* * * * *

Stephen F. Austin died in Columbia on December 27, 1836, after a cold developed into pneumonia. Austin was serving as Secretary of State at the time of his death. Austin was only 43.

* * * * *

The town of Columbia, where the first Congress of the Republic convened, is now **West Columbia**. A replica of the building used by Congress was built in 1977.

* * * * *

Waxahachie is the **Movie Capital of Texas**. More than twenty major motion pictures and made-for-TV movies have been filmed in and around the area in the last three years. Movie production began in 1967 with the filming of *Bonnie & Clyde*.

* * * * *

The name **Waxahachie** is from an Indian word meaning "Buffalo Creek" or "Cow Creek."

* * * * *

The first president of Texas A&M University was **Sul Ross**, Captain of the Texas Rangers, a Confederate general, state senator, and governor of Texas from 1886 to 1890.

* * * * *

In 1991 the State Legislature named **Parker County** the Peach Capital of Texas.

* * * * *

Yoakum is the **Leather Capital** of the Southwest and is known as "The Land of Leather."

* * * * *

Did you know that when **Falcon Lake** filled with water, the original towns of Zapata, Ramireno, Lopeno, and Falcon were covered over? These towns relocated to their present locations on higher ground. The International Falcon Dam, across the Rio Grande River, was started December 15, 1950 and was completed on April 8, 1954. It was dedicated on October 19, 1953 by President Dwight D. Eisenhower.

* * * * *

Zapata, the county seat of Zapata County is unincorporated.

* * * * *

Did you know that **Wylie** used to be called Nickleville?

* * * * *

Wimberley is unhurried and peaceful, nestled in a valley near Austin and San Antonio. The slower pace can be shown by the fact that only a few homes had electricity in 1949 and only 350 homes had phones by 1968. Wimberly is growing, but it doesn't seem to mind taking its time to let the outside world come in.

* * * * *

Driftwood, once known as the Liberty Hill Community, was renamed in 1885 when driftwood kept washing up after the area creeks flooded.

* * * * *

Woodville is the Dogwood Capital of Texas.

* * * * *

Did you know that there is a town called **Dam B** east of Woodville in Tyler County? The community is located on the shores of B.S. Steinhagen Lake. The dam which formed the lake was called "Dam B" since it was to be the second dam built. The first dam on the plans, Dam A, was never built. The community that grew up around the dam took on its nickname and is still called Dam B, Texas.

* * * * *

Chapter 4 ————————————————

Special Stops

Park headquarters at Rusk State Park

The **Luling Watermelon Thump** is held downtown the last Thursday, Friday, and Saturday of June each year. You need to go and participate in the Guinness record-setting seed spitting contests. The 1989 seed spitting record is 68 feet 9 1/8 inches and was set by Lee Wheelis. Even though the first place prize is $500, another $500 bonus will be awarded to the first person breaking the record.

* * * * *

Do you have a taste for the spicy? Go to Farmers Branch in July for the **Jalapeno Festival** which includes a cornbread cookoff—got to have something to go with those hot little things!

* * * * *

The 19th **Annual World Champion Barbecue Goat Cook-Off** was held in Brady in September 1992. Not all of the activities were for the grownups—if you were 8 and under you could pan for gold. I think we need to write and get the age limit raised!

* * * * *

Blue Bell Creameries, founded in 1907 as Brenham Creamery Co., only produced two gallons of ice cream a day in 1911. The creamery, located in Brenham, now produces 20 million gallons a year. Free tours Monday through Friday . . . good stuff, but why not try it for yourself!

* * * * *

Cave Without a Name is the actual name of the cave opened in 1939. When the cave opened, a contest was held to name the cave and a small boy won the contest when he said "This cave is too pretty to name."

* * * * *

On November 21, 1831, Jim Bowie and 10 others held 164 Indians off at **Calf Creek**. After 80 Indians were killed, the rest retreated. The Bowie Battleground Monument is at Brady.

* * * * *

Andrews Prairie Dog Town Camper Park, in **Andrews**, provides free overnight parking and utilities for visitors with travel trailers. The accommodations include electrical, water, and sewer connections. This is a great way to get people to stop and see the area!

* * * * *

Ever wonder what is on the food you buy at the grocery store and wonder what you can do about it? The **Natural Food Associates** farm in Atlanta has tours and demonstrations on organic methods of producing crops and livestock.

* * * * *

If you like art, **4000-year-old rock art** should be of interest to you. The paintings are located in an old Indian cave shelter, in Seminole Canyon State Park, approximately 20 miles east of Langtry. The artwork can be reached by guided hiking tours.

* * * * *

The state's electric chair, known as "**Old Sparky**," was used between 1924 and 1964. It is now on display at the Texas Prison Museum in Houston.

* * * * *

The original **Alamo bell**, cast in 1722, is among the historical relics at the Nita Stewart Haley Memorial Library—J. Evetts Haley History Center in Midland. Over 10,000 items are in the collection on display with the emphasis being on Texas and Southwestern history.

* * * * *

If you know someone who loves music boxes, take them to Sulphur Springs. The **Music Box Gallery** is housed in the library and has a collection of more than 150 boxes. The collection was started in 1919 by Leo St. Clair when he received a music box from the Belgian royal family.

* * * * *

Dungeons and gallows in Texas? Try the old jail in Gonzales. The old jail built in 1887 was in use until 1975. The jail has been restored—complete with dungeon and gallows.

* * * * *

Where would you look for the world's largest collection of Texas Longhorn steer horns? Go to the **Heritage Museum** in Big Spring. Before you leave, make sure you see the exhibit of 46 phonographs dating from the late 1800s to 1920 made by Edison, Victor, Columbia, and others.

* * * * *

For the child in all of us, the **Bauer Toy Museum** in Fredericksburg displays toy soldiers, fire trucks, airplane replicas, and other smaller toys of times past.

* * * * *

A vast collection of police memorabilia dating back to the turn of the century can be seen at the **Beaumont Police Museum**.

* * * * *

One sure fact of life is death, but if you want to see how it was handled in bygone years, make a stop at the **Van Alstyne Museum**. Not only does the museum feature a 1880s horse-drawn buggy, but it has equipment used by early undertakers, old caskets, grave liners, and cooling boards!

* * * * *

The largest shell collection in the Southwest can be found in the **Brazosport Museum of Natural Science** in Clute. The museum also has an aquarium and collections of fossils and minerals on display.

* * * * *

The **Museum of Texas Handmade Furniture** displays furniture pieces handcrafted in Texas in the 1800s. The museum occupies a home built in 1858 in New Braunfels.

* * * * *

Yes, there is an Easter elephant. The prehistoric mammoth found in 1988, near Easter, is now located in the **Llano Estacado Museum** in Plainview.

* * * * *

Brewer's Bells Museum in Canton contains about 3,200 bells.

* * * * *

A collection of **branding irons and barbed wire** can be seen in the Kleberg Center at Texas A&M University.

* * * * *

Los Nogales Museum in Seguin was built by the Mexican government for use as a post office in 1823.

* * * * *

The **Sewing Machine Museum** in Arlington displays over 90 vintage machines dating from 1858 to 1935. The museum even has an old treadle machine the children are allowed to use.

* * * * *

The **International Kite Museum**, in Corpus Christi, tells the story of kites from Chinese kites of 2000 years ago, to kites used in scientific discoveries in recent years.

* * * * *

Yes, there is more than one kind of barbed wire. To see a collection go to the **Knox County Museum** in Benjamin.

* * * * *

A moon rock is on display at the **Lyndon B. Johnson Library and Museum** in Austin.

* * * * *

The Paluxy dinosaur tracks can be seen at the **Texas Memorial Museum** in Austin.

* * * * *

The fur parka worn by Admiral Richard E. Byrd during the first flight to the South Pole in 1929 is located in the **Frontiers of Flight Museum** in Dallas. Also on display are items from the Hindenberg crash.

* * * * *

The *Gossamer Penguin*, the first solar-powered aircraft, is on exhibit in the **Science Place I** in Dallas.

* * * * *

The **Air Defense & Artillery Museum** in El Paso is the only one of its kind in the country.

* * * * *

Fort Bend County Historical Museum has a special exhibit on local resident Jane Long, "the mother of Texas."

* * * * *

The Texas prison system was started in 1848, and the changes that the system has gone through are recorded at the **Texas Prison Museum** in Huntsville.

* * * * *

The **Franks Antique Doll Museum** in Marshall has over 1600 dolls in its collection along with doll furniture, buggies, trunks, dishes, and much more.

* * * * *

The Great Southwest Golf Course, in Grand Prairie, has **gold in the sand traps**—not very much, but it is there—about $2 per ton of sand.

* * * * *

There are only a few **sugar refineries** remaining in the U.S., but visitors to the Imperial Holly Sugar Co., in Sugar Land, can take a weekday tour to see the complete sugar manufacturing process.

* * * * *

The **Marion West Blakemore Planetarium** in Midland conducts sky shows for the public throughout the year. During the school year, the planetarium is used by the Midland schools for astronomy classes.

* * * * *

Have you ever seen a **15-inch horse**? The miniature horses can be seen at the St. Clare Monastery Miniature Horse Farm in Brenham.

* * * * *

If you have the courage, **Comanche Peak Nuclear Power Plant**, in Glen Rose, conducts tours of the plant site.

* * * * *

The Garden Center at Tyrrell Park in Beaumont has a special "**touch and smell**" garden for the blind.

* * * * *

Need a rest? Stop in at one of the more than **one thousand rest areas** along Texas roads, but don't stay longer than 24 hours or put up any kind of structure; these two things are prohibited.

* * * * *

Need a snack before going on your way? Be sure to stop at the Puddin' Hill Bakery in **Greenville**. Known for its world famous fruitcake and chocolates, you can stop and have samples or soup and sandwiches. Located on I-30.

* * * * *

Are you a star gazer, or know one, or just dream of being on board a star ship going to the outer reaches of the galaxy? Make reservations with the visitors center of the University of Texas McDonald Observatory at Mount Locke for a once-a-month chance for amateur astronomers to view celestial objects through a **107-inch telescope**. Sometimes this treat is booked months in advance, so make your plans early to go to the Fort Davis area.

* * * * *

If you are in Devine, go by the **Stroud blacksmith shop**. The shop has been in continuous operation since 1903, and especially notice the doors. There are hundreds of cattle brands burned into the doors—the ones the shop has made over the years.

* * * * *

Downtown **Crystal City** proudly displays a statue of Popeye—the town is famous for its spinach crop.

* * * * *

Weid Hardware, in **Cameron,** has been operating since the 1880s.

* * * * *

Cascade Cavern is an active cave with a 90-foot underground waterfall. The cave northwest of San Antonio has been a popular attraction since 1932.

* * * * *

In **Pearsall** there is a giant statue of a peanut to honor the millions of pounds of peanuts that are harvested there each year.

* * * * *

Aransas Pass has a 19-foot statue of a shrimp.

* * * * *

If you want to tour a candle factory, try the one in **Georgetown**. The factory produces more than a thousand kinds of decorative candles, and visitors are welcome.

* * * * *

Texas' newest cavern is called **Inner Space** in Georgetown off of Interstate 35. The temperature in the cave stays at an average 72 degrees all year long. The cave has beautiful features and remains of prehistoric animals.

* * * * *

Nocona is famed as the "Leathergoods Center of the Southwest." The Nocona Boot Co. displays boot-making tools from the 1890s.

* * * * *

The **West Texas Fair** is held for 10 days in mid-September in Abilene.

* * * * *

Belton has been striving to preserve the historic structures in the downtown area. Some of these buildings and homes are opened during the annual tour in late April and early May.

* * * * *

The **Norse community**, near Clifton, celebrates their customs each November, dressed in national Norse costumes, by enjoying a giant smorgasbord.

* * * * *

The **National Polka Festival** is held in May in Ennis.

* * * * *

October is the time for the **annual chili festival** or Czhilispiel celebrated by the Czechs in Flatonia.

* * * * *

General Sam Houston Folk Festival in April is held in Huntsville.

* * * * *

Jacksonville celebrates the **Tomato Fest** in September.

* * * * *

Kerrville is the home of the **Texas State Arts & Crafts Fair**, Memorial Day weekend.

* * * * *

Laredo holds a 10-day fiesta, celebrated on both sides of the border, honoring George Washington as the first Western Hemisphere leader to free a New World country from European rule. The **Washington Birthday Celebration** has been celebrated since 1898.

* * * * *

Panhandle-South Plains Fair is held in Lubbock the last week in September and is one of the largest regional fairs in the state.

* * * * *

Mule Day is the second Saturday in August in Muleshoe. The celebration consists of a mule rodeo and mule races.

* * * * *

Mesquite hosts a **hot air balloonfest** in July each year for balloons from all over the U.S.

* * * * *

If you want to see lumberjacks at work, go to Atlanta for the **Texas Forest Festival** around the middle of August. The festival celebrations include a forest skill contest for the lumberjacks.

* * * * *

Plano has become known as the "Balloon Capital of Texas" with hot air balloon races the last weekend in September.

* * * * *

The **Strawberry Festival** is held in early April in Poteet.

* * * * *

If you like chili, and what Texan doesn't, you need to witness the world's largest bowl of chili at the **Chili Super Bowl**. It is held in Abilene on Labor Day weekend in September, with two days of chili and brisket cook-offs.

* * * * *

Abilene is the place to be if you like kite flying. The last weekend in September the annual **Wind Festival** features kite contests and exhibits.

* * * * *

Aransas Pass holds the annual "**Shrimporee**" in September, which is only fitting since Aransas Pass is the Shrimp Capital of the World. The world's largest and most modern shrimping facilities are at Conn Brown Harbor, home of the shrimp fleet, which accommodates up to 500 vessels.

* * * * *

Did you know the small town of **Bloomburg**, population 200, grows overnight to over 10,000 people during the Cullen Baker Country Fair. I've been told this is not one to be missed; obviously there are a lot of people who feel this way!

* * * * *

Where do you go for a **coon hunt**? The Cystic Fibrosis Coon Hunt is held in Atlanta.

* * * * *

If you want to see parts of the Palo Duro Canyon that you can't get to by car, catch the **Sad Monkey Railroad**. This railroad features miniature train cars and a two-mile narrated tour—very scenic and colorful.

* * * * *

The Panhandle-Plains Historical Museum in Canyon is the **largest state supported museum** in Texas. It contains western art, artifacts, and the history of the petroleum industry.

* * * * *

The **Annual Black-Eyed Pea Jamboree** in Athens is held the third weekend in July for three days, celebrating the fact that Athens is the Black-Eyed Pea Capital of the World. There are pea cooking, pea eating, pea popping, and pea shelling contests. By the way, the pea cooking contest usually has 100 entrants trying for a part of the $3000 prize money. Got any good recipes?

* * * * *

If you get to go to the Black-Eyed Pea Jamboree in Athens and you get tired of the peas, there is a watermelon eating contest and a **NATO 500 Gran Prix Terrapin Race**.

* * * * *

Yes, there is a fiddler statue on the Henderson County courthouse lawn. Since the early 1900s the **Old Fiddler's Contest and Reunion** has been held the last Friday in May on the courthouse lawn in Athens.

* * * * *

If you are in Austin in August, take off your shoes—for the **Grape Stomp**! Join in the tradition of wine making and the stompin' of the grapes. No admission, just a lot of fun and food.

* * * * *

The **Gatorfest** in Anahuac in September is held at the same time as the alligator hunting season—no thanks!

* * * * *

Most of us worry about our cholesterol—but not in Kountze in November! They hold the **Great Texas Crackling Cookout**. You don't know what cracklings are? Crispy fried fat—you take lots of chunks of pork fat, fry them up till the grease is cooked out, squeeze the rest of the grease out in a press, and enjoy to your heart's content. Actually, I've done this as a little girl and have made myself sick eating the cracklings!

* * * * *

Beaumont is known as the **Museum Capital of Texas**, with 19 museums within its city limits.

* * * * *

The **Edison Plaza Museum** in Beaumont has one of the largest collections of Thomas Edison's inventions and the advances he made in electricity.

* * * * *

The Apple Capital of Texas is **Medina**, and in the spring they celebrate with an annual Texas International Apple Festival.

* * * * *

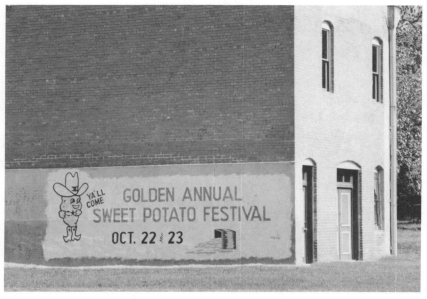

The annual Sweet Potato Festival is held in Golden each year to celebrate the area's main crop. Golden is located in East Texas north of the Grand Saline/Mineola area.

The **Frontier Times Museum** in Bandera has a collection of 400 bells from all parts of the world—part of the Louisa Gordon collection. There are Russian sleigh bells, elephant bells, camel bells, and Chinese temple bells; the oldest bell in the collection is a gong from China's Han dynasty dated between 207 B.C. to A.D. 220. The museum also has Old West relics, Indian artifacts, and Buffalo Bill Wild West Show posters. A different sort of collection.

* * * * *

Did you know the **Sam Rayburn Library**, in Bonham, houses a 2500-year-old Grecian urn? The urn was presented to the Speaker by the Athens Palace Guard—Athens, Greece, that is.

* * * * *

Every year in **Forestburg** they have a community Thanksgiving meal, a potluck dinner, the last Thursday before Thanksgiving Day.

* * * * *

The **Fort Croghan Museum** in Burnet has a ballot box that was used in 1852 and a dental "do-it-yourself" kit—ouch!

* * * * *

Bridge City holds the International Mayhaw Mania Conference and Festival in April each year to promote the production of the mayhaw berry.

* * * * *

Chappell Hill has celebrated the **Scarecrow Festival** since 1977. During the month of October, the homes and businesses are decorated with scarecrows, and on festival weekend they celebrate by blocking off the main street for exhibitors, cooking contests, and hayrides.

* * * * *

The **Maifest**, celebrated in May in Brenham, enjoyed its 103rd anniversary in 1993. The Maifestival is an old fashioned German folk festival.

* * * * *

The Douglas MacArthur Academy of Freedom, in **Brownwood**, specializes in history and government. The school is dedicated to General Douglas MacArthur and displays some of his personal souvenirs. The school also has an exact replica of Philadelphia's Independence Hall.

* * * * *

The city of **Columbus** was designated as the official Quincentennial town of Texas for the national celebration, in 1992, commemorating the 500th anniversary of Christopher Columbus's voyage. The town really wasn't named after Columbus. The story is told about a surveyor who helped plat the town in 1823. He had come through Columbus, Ohio, and suggested Columbus as the town's new name.

* * * * *

Caldwell holds its annual **Kolache Festival** the second Saturday of September. The kolache was originally a Czech wedding pastry, but it is a favorite national dessert throughout Czechoslovakia. The immigrants brought the kolache with them, and it is celebrated with the festival and the Burleson County Champion and State Champion Kolache Baker contests.

* * * * *

Laguna Park has **Texas' Largest Fish Fry** the Saturday before Labor Day.

* * * * *

Sweetwater holds their annual **World's Largest Rattlesnake Roundup** in March.

* * * * *

There is an annual **$125,000 Big Bass Tournament** in Conroe.

* * * * *

Corpus Christi has become the unofficial **windsurfing** capital of the continental U.S. The average wind speed in Corpus Christi is 12 miles per hour, making it one of the consistently windiest cities in the country.

* * * * *

Did you know the **Rockport-Fulton** area has a festival devoted to hummingbirds?

* * * * *

Like to build sandcastles at the beach? You need to go to the annual **Texas Crab Festival** at Crystal Beach in May and enter the sandcastle contest.

* * * * *

The **Galveston-Bolivar Ferry**, a free state-operated ferry, makes the three-mile trip often accompanied by dolphins. There are four ferries. The three smaller ones weigh 588 tons and can carry about 69 cars each. The larger ferry, called the *Gibb Gilchrist*, can carry

85 cars. The ferry ride takes about 15 minutes and there is a ferry leaving about every 20 minutes.

* * * * *

The *Selma* was an **experimental concrete ship** built during World War I. The ship sank in 1922 and her remains can be seen sticking out of the water in the bay between Galveston Island and the Bolivar Peninsula.

* * * * *

Yoakum Heritage Museum sponsors the annual **Christmas Tree Forest**, more than 80 decorated trees for everyone to enjoy!

* * * * *

The **Tom Tom Festival**, the first weekend in June in Yoakum, celebrates the tomato. The festival was first held as a project of the Chamber of Commerce. The Chamber encouraged the farmers to grow tomatoes in 1925 as an extra money crop because the area economy had slowed. Three years later, the tomato crops were a huge success and the first Tom Tom Festival was held in 1928.

* * * * *

There are ten **leather factories** in Yoakum and most host a daily tour, and some of the factories have retail outlets. Now that is a Texan's shopping dream—to be let loose in a leather factory!

* * * * *

Christmas in Goliad is pure Texan—Santa arrives at the festivities in a **longhorn-drawn sleigh**! Only in Texas!

* * * * *

The **Texas State Championship Domino Hall of Fame** is in Hallettsville. Hallettsville is known for its domino halls, and the town hosts the State Championship Domino Tournament in January and the State Championship 42 Tournament in March.

* * * * *

Want something different in the way of celebrations? Go to Victoria in October for the International Armadillo Confab & Exposition. This is a two-day event which has contests like: The Miss Vacant Lot of the World and Surrounding Counties Extravaganza—**The Jalapeno Gobble—Ice Cream Lick-off** (bet you this follows the jalapeno contest!)—Armadillo Races and the Whimmy Diddle Off (you just have to be there!).

* * * * *

Remember when we could go to the drive-in? Seems like all the drive-ins have disappeared. If you would like to take the kids, try the **Brazos Old Fashioned Drive-In Theater** in Granbury. Bring the lawn chairs and cooler and enjoy one of Texas' few remaining drive-in theaters.

* * * * *

Over **160 museums and galleries** make Dallas their home.

Texas State Railroad Engine 500—restored and ready. The Texas State Railroad operates several restored engines and train cars along the "longest and skinniest state park in the U.S." between Rusk and Palestine.

* * * * *

In April **Traders Village**, in Grand Prairie, hosts its Annual Prairie Dog Chili Cook-Off and World Championship of Pickled Quail Egg Eating. Hummmmm. . . . .

* * * * *

The **first pecan show** held in Texas was at Eastland, and each year the show is still held in early December.

* * * * *

If you ask any Texan, the most terrible pest that we have to put up with is the fire ant. Even though it is imported, it likes Texas as well as we do, with no intention of leaving. We have done almost everything to eradicate the varmint, but its armies keep multiplying, advancing, and attacking! The people of Marshall got tired of the fight and started celebrating with the **Fire Ant Festival** in October—if you can't beat them, have a party!

* * * * *

Why go to New Orleans for Mardi Gras? Go to Galveston Island in February for their celebration of **Mardi Gras** when the whole island parties in the streets.

* * * * *

Don't miss the **Sling Shot Derby** in Paris in May.

* * * * *

The first weekend in May, Ennis celebrates its rich Czechoslovakian heritage each year with the **National Polka Festival**. The city of Ennis and the surrounding area make up one of the largest Czechoslovakian settlements in Texas.

* * * * *

Gish's Old West Museum in Fredericksburg houses a complete display of Old West relics including saddles, lawmen's badges, and old guns. The collection displays items from 1870 to 1920.

* * * * *

The *Pride of Galveston* is the **largest cruise ship** in Texas, docked at Pier 21 at the Port of Galveston, the ship offers day and evening cruises with the excitement of a Las Vegas casino on board.

* * * * *

There are only 10 original **hobby horse carousels** in the world. If you want to see one of these, go to Giddings. The carousels operate on special occasions and the horses date back to the early 1900s.

The Giddings Volunteer Fire Department is responsible for the renovation and the continued maintenance of the carousel.

* * * * *

The National Cowgirl Hall of Fame and Western Heritage Center is in **Hereford**. A magazine is published giving news and history of the museum—it is called *Sidesaddle.*

* * * * *

Hempstead claims to be "Watermelon Capital of the World" and on the third Saturday in July, you can take part in the Annual Watermelon Festival.

* * * * *

On the second Saturday in December, Santa and Pancho Claus come to **Hondo,** and the whole town celebrates with a downtown Christmas party.

* * * * *

The **Cowboy Artists of America Museum** is in Kerrville. The Cowboy Artists of America is made up of the nation's best living Western artists, who are chosen to be a part of the association. Not just any artist can join.

* * * * *

If you need a place to camp in **Winkler County,** go by the county judge's office. You can make arrangements to stay in one of the 12 Winkler County campsites, with hook-ups, for up to three days, at no charge. Of course this is on a first come, first serve basis.

* * * * *

Lufkin holds a week-long **Texas Forest Festival** the third week of September, which includes the Southern Hushpuppy Olympics with $1000 in prize money.

* * * * *

The **Great Texas Balloon Race** in Longview on the 4th of July determines the Texas Champion.

* * * * *

In May, **Longview** is besieged with hundreds of fishermen coming to take part in the "World's Largest/Richest Big Bass Contest," the KYKX Big Bass Classic.

* * * * *

Marshall is known for its **Christmas lights**. With over 4.5 million lights throughout the city, it is the nation's largest light show. The

45-foot Christmas tree on the square has over 9,000 red, white, and blue lights and is topped with three stars. The Wonderland of Lights is held annually between Thanksgiving and New Years Day.

* * * * *

The **Muy Grande Deer Contest**, said to be the world's largest deer contest, was started in 1966 as a marketing ploy to get people to stop at Leonel R. Garza's gas station in Freer. The annual contest, held during hunting season in November, attracts celebrities and people from all over the country.

* * * * *

Did you know that the **National Cow Calling Contest and Old Timers' Reunion** is held each year in Miami? The cow calling contest was first held in 1949 and still goes on today.

* * * * *

The first **Blueberry Festival** in Nacogdoches was held in June 1992, and a 2,022-foot blueberry strudel made there is listed in the Buinness Book of World Records as the world's longest.

* * * * *

The **Presidential Museum** in Odessa is the only museum in the country dedicated to the office of the President. In the museum is the Dishong collection of First Lady Dolls which authentically document the Inaugural Balls.

* * * * *

The **Globe of the Great Southwest**, a recreation of Shakespeare's original Globe Theatre, is located in Odessa, on Shakespeare Road.

* * * * *

The **Annual Potato Festival** is held in Pearsall the first weekend in June. Which potato are they celebrating? They have an abundance of both Irish and sweet potatoes. Which do you prefer?

* * * * *

The **Hot Pepper Festival & County Fair** is held the last full weekend in October in Palestine. Part of the activities is a firemen muster. Bet they need it with the hot peppers!

* * * * *

The **Old Clock Museum** in Pharr consists of over 1650 very old antique clocks and music boxes. The majority of these items are in good working order. There are only five museums in the country like this one. Any donations made by the museum visitors are given to charity.

* * * * *

Did you know the **Gulf blue marlin** record is 876 pounds? The Texas International Fishing Tournament, held in August, has been pulling in the big ones for over 50 years.

* * * * *

The **longest bridge** in Texas is supposed to be the causeway at Port Isabel. Ordinarily you are not allowed to walk across the causeway, but in October you can participate in the annual Causeway Run and Wellness Walk.

* * * * *

The Texas Electric Railway connected Denison with Dallas and Waco from 1908 to 1948. **The Interurban Station in Plano** has been restored as a museum, complete with one of the original electric cars, #360, believed to be only one of three that have been restored in the U.S.

* * * * *

The 4th of July has been celebrated in **Round Top** since the 1820s, but documented proof starts the festivities in 1851. Round Top's celebration of Independence Day has been going on longer than any other city west of the Mississippi River.

* * * * *

After the Battle of San Jacinto, Joel W. Robinson was presented a small chest containing some of General Santa Anna's personal things. This was a gift in gratitude for his kindness while Santa Anna was held captive. A **braided vest** with gold buttons was one of the items in the chest, and it became customary for the young men of Round Top to wear the vest on their wedding day.

* * * * *

The Richmond State School, in Richmond, hosts a 140-acre display of larger-than-life lighted scenes during the holiday season, called **Project Noel**.

* * * * *

San Antonio was the site of the 1968 World's Fair. At the time of the fair, the Old San Antonio River was extended into the fairgrounds and waterfalls were added. The **Tower of the Americas**, located at HemisFair Park, is the nation's tallest free standing structure. The

Institute of Texan Cultures, also in the park, presents the story of the Texas people to visitors.

* * * * *

Did you know that the **Hertzberg Circus Collection** in San Antonio includes Tom Thumb's miniature coach? The museum has a collection of circus memorabilia from the time of King Charles II to the era of P.T. Barnum.

* * * * *

For one day a year the San Antonio River is dyed green and renamed the **River Shannon**. When is this one day? Why around St. Patrick's Day, when else. It is not always on March 17, so check San Antonio's calendar of events for the exact day of the St. Patrick's River Dyeing.

* * * * *

During one week in January of each year, the San Antonio River Walk is drained for maintenance. A **Mud King and Queen** help lighten the spirits during this depressing period of a river without water.

* * * * *

The city of Seymour has the only "**Fish Day**" holiday in the nation. Held the first weekend in May, the celebration lasts three days. The whole town closes up shop and heads for Lake Kemp. Only the U.S. government offices stay open.

* * * * *

On the courthouse square in Snyder, a **white buffalo statue** stands. On October 7, 1876, J. Wright Mooar killed a rare white albino buffalo in this area. Mr. Mooar killed another white buffalo in Kansas before the one in Snyder. There have only been seven or eight albino buffaloes killed in the U.S.

* * * * *

The **Texas Cowboy Reunion**, held annually in July in Stamford, is known as the largest amateur rodeo in the world—based on the number of contestants.

* * * * *

The annual **Oysterfest** in Fulton is held during the first of March with men and women's raw oyster eating contests.

* * * * *

Want to do something different for a friend's birthday? Go to Temple to the Railroad & Pioneer Museum and **rent a caboose** for the party. Last time we checked, the caboose party rental fee was $25.

* * * * *

Rhonesboro, west of Gilmer, celebrates the **Possum Festival** in October. Rhonesboro is the home of the International Possum Museum.

* * * * *

The **East Texas Yamboree** is one of the oldest continuing festivals in Texas, established in 1935. The celebration is held in Gilmer in October.

* * * * *

The **Caverns of Sonora**, located about seven miles from Sonora, contain a "butterfly" formation which no other cave is known to have. The caverns were discovered by a shepherd around the turn of the century and in July 1960 were opened to the public. The Caverns of Sonora have more "helectites" than all of the other known caverns in the world put together. Helectites are limestone formations that grow out of the walls forming loops, horseshoes, and elk's horns. Some of the "soda straw" formations in the caverns are up to six feet long and are some of the largest known.

* * * * *

Want to do some "dam sliding"? Try the **Ingram Dam** at Ingram Lake. The local sport is sliding down the slick wall of the dam!

* * * * *

Port Arthur has a **two-acre white sand beach**. The sand was imported from the Grand Bahamas!

* * * * *

Built in 1902, the Waxahachie Chautauqua Auditorium, an **octagonal amphitheater**, is the only one of its kind in Texas and only one of three in the nation, possibly the only one that remains standing today. Built at a cost of $1500, it cost $200,000 to restore in 1972 when the town voted to use its restoration as a Bicentennial project.

* * * * *

The **Texas Ranger Museum** in Waco tells the history of the Rangers from 1823 to the present. Jim Bowie's knife is on display.

* * * * *

The largest collection in the world of Elizabeth and Robert Browning related materials is in Waco on the Baylor campus. Fifty-one stained glass windows illustrate the poems of the Brownings in the **Armstrong-Browning Library**. This group of stained glass windows is believed to be the largest secular collection in the world.

* * * * *

The **Heritage Museum** in Yoakum contains a collection of unique leather products from the area's leather companies.

* * * * *

Yoakum sponsors the **Land of Leather Days** the last weekend of February. Yoakum is known for its handcrafted leather products with ten leather companies located there. The celebration centers around a famous Chili Cook-Off.

* * * * *

The **World Championship Stone Skipping Contest** is held the second weekend in October on the banks of the Cypress Creek in Wimberley.

* * * * *

The Allan Shivers Library & Museum is in Woodville. **Allan Shivers** was governor of Texas from 1949 to 1957—longer than any other Texas governor has served.

* * * * *

Tyler County celebrates their annual **Dogwood Festival** the first weekend in April. The festival has been held since the mid-1930s.

* * * * *

The Heritage Village Museum, in Woodville, is the site for the **Tyler County Blacksmith Association Annual Hammerfest**.

* * * * *

Lake McQueeney claims to be the Water Ski Capital of Texas. The lake is located five miles northwest of Seguin.

* * * * *

More than nine million visitors come to **Lake Texoma** each year.

* * * * *

Monahans Sandhills State Park features 4,000 acres of sand dunes and one of the popular activities is **sand surfing**.

* * * * *

Chapter 5 ————————————

Farm and Ranch— Cowboys and Indians

During the **Civil War**, Texas was supposed to have nine cattle for every resident in the state.

* * * * *

Quanah Parker took the last name of his white mother. He led the Comanches as one of their principal war chiefs until his surrender in 1875. Realizing that resistance would only destroy his people, Quanah helped the Comanches to adapt to their new surroundings and the white ways. He became the main spokesman for the Indians on the reservation in Oklahoma. Before his death he had his mother's body moved from Texas to a family cemetery next to his ranch. Two weeks later Quanah Parker died and was buried next to his mother. A spear-shaped cedar tree was planted at the head of his grave, pointing the way to Heaven—a Comanche custom.

* * * * *

Did you know the **American Quarter Horse Association** is the largest horse registry in the world? More than 2.6 million horses are registered in 53 countries. The Quarter Horse was the first American horse breed. The American Quarter Horse Association's headquarters are in Amarillo, and in June of 1991, they opened their new Heritage Center & Museum that houses the American Quarter Horse Hall of Fame.

* * * * *

Within Palo Duro Canyon State Park is a historical marker citing the **last great Indian battle** in Texas in 1874.

* * * * *

The nation's largest **all-girl rodeo** takes place in late summer in Hereford.

* * * * *

According to legend, **Spider Mountain** near Burnet was an Indian burial ground.

* * * * *

Three million cattle a year go through feedlots in the **Hereford** area, which was named for early herds of Hereford cattle.

* * * * *

The first breed of cattle developed in the Western Hemisphere was the **Santa Gertrudis** on the King Ranch in Kingsville.

* * * * *

The **longest fenced cattle trail** in the world once stretched from Brady to Sonora, 250 feet wide and 100 miles long, purchased and fenced by the Fort Worth & Rio Grande Railroad.

* * * * *

Prehistoric Caddo Indian villages have been discovered in the area of **Atlanta**.

* * * * *

The **King Ranch** in Kingsville is the largest ranch in the continental U.S. Established in 1853 with 75,000 acres, the King Ranch now consists of 825,000 acres, covers more than 1300 square miles, and is larger than the entire state of Rhode Island.

* * * * *

Ysleta del Sur Pueblo, **Tigua Indian Reservation**, is the oldest community in the present boundaries of Texas and now part of the city of El Paso.

* * * * *

The **Texas Hereford Association** had its first sale of purebred stock on March 1, 1922 in Sweetwater.

* * * * *

Did you know that 75% of Texas' cattle feedyards are located in the **Amarillo area**?

* * * * *

The **Amarillo Livestock Auction** is the largest in Texas. They sell over 300,000 head of cattle each year. If you want to experience it yourself, the auction is held year round every Tuesday at the Western Stockyards, but be sure you know what you are doing or you could end up with a 'little doggie' to bring home!

* * * * *

East of Athens is the **Black Beauty Ranch**. The ranch takes in abused and unwanted animals—of an equine nature. The tour is free, but you may lose your heart.

* * * * *

Bandera is the Cowboy Capital of the World.

* * * * *

* * * * *

Comanche is known as the "Peanut Capital of the World." Comanche County processes over 51 million pounds of peanuts annually.

* * * * *

Munday is now known as the Vegetable Capital of North Texas and is home to the **Texas A&M Vegetable Research Station**.

* * * * *

Over one million pounds of **wool** are clipped annually in Coleman County—the fourth largest sheep producing county in Texas.

* * * * *

Dude ranches were established in Bandera County beginning in 1920 with the Buck Ranch and the Bruce Ranch taking in vacation boarders. By the early 1940s there were 24 or so dude ranches.

* * * * *

Tobacco grown at Willis won first prize at the Columbian World's Exposition in Chicago in 1893 and at Paris in 1900.

* * * * *

In 1880, 40 thousand tons of steel **barbed wire** were sold to Texas cattlemen.

* * * * *

Mr. George Copp, an Englishman in La Salle County, planted the first **Bermuda onions** in 1895, and in 1896 he was shipping the first onion plants in Texas. By 1900 the Bermuda onion crop had become an important industry to the area.

* * * * *

The Refugio County courthouse has a collection of over 200 **cattle brands**—burned in leather.

* * * * *

The **Beefmaster** breed of cattle was started in Falfurrias, in Brooks County.

* * * * *

In 1987 Floydada claimed the title **"Pumpkin Capital USA."** In 1990, 23 million pounds of pumpkins were shipped from the Floydada area to every part of the country. The harvest is celebrated on the last weekend of October with "Punkin' Days."

* * * * *

Open spaces and barbed wire have become symbols of the Texas way of life. Skyscrapers, concrete, and the hustle-bustle of city life can never compare with the feeling of freedom that this photo displays.

Pastures, oak trees, and cattle still are the way of life for many ranching families in Texas.

The first **Agricultural Experiment Substation** in Texas was established in Bee County in 1894. The research station is on 450 acres and is now operating under the Gulf Coast Research Complex with headquarters in Corpus Christi.

* * * * *

Texas is the second largest **agricultural producer** in the nation, and agriculture is the state's second largest industry.

* * * * *

Washington County is the Horse Capital of Texas.

* * * * *

The top-ranked feeder **pig market** in Texas is Washington County. In 1988 they sold over 45,000 pigs.

* * * * *

The **Stan Guffey Memorial Jr. Rodeo** is known as the "Super Bowl of the Nation." This four-night event is held in Brady in memory of Texas Ranger Stan Guffey, who was killed in the line of duty.

* * * * *

Leon County is ranked second in Texas for the number of beef cattle, with approximately 87,000 head.

* * * * *

The **Texas Cattle Raisers' Association** was organized February 1877 in Graham, under an oak tree at Fourth and Oak streets! The oak was destroyed by storms in the 1970s.

* * * * *

In 1898 the town of **Blue Water** changed its name to Hereford, named for a herd of Hereford cattle that had just been brought to Deaf Smith County by Mr. G.R. Jowell. This is cattle country—and this proves it!

* * * * *

The **aloe industry** got its start in Texas in 1939 by Mrs. Lee Ewald, who established Hilltop Gardens near La Villa. The Rio Grande Valley grows more aloe vera than any other area of the U.S.

* * * * *

In 1930 the U.S. Department of Agriculture established an **entomology station** in Kerrville. This station was used for the breeding and research of screwworm flies that resulted in their eradication in the U.S.

* * * * *

The **first Texas cattle drive** on record was from old Anahuac to New Orleans during the late 1830s headed up by James Taylor White.

* * * * *

J.C. Turner, Sr. was the first Texan to import **Jersey cattle**.

* * * * *

The **prickly pear cactus'** fruit sells for $4 to $5 a pound and of all things is called "tuna." The fruit, and the cactus pads, is one of the latest crops to be experimented with in Texas. Why not? The people of Texas have walked 'way around' it for years, why not use it for food and cattle feed?

* * * * *

State supported agricultural science began at Troup in 1902, with the first Texas A&M experimental station.

* * * * *

Llano is the Deer Capital of Texas. Did you know that the deer concentration is greater in the Llano Basin than in any other area of the country.

* * * * *

Laredo became known as the Bermuda onion capital of the U.S. in 1900.

* * * * *

Memphis is the Cotton Capital of the Panhandle.

* * * * *

The **Boys Corn Club**, the forerunner to the 4-H Club, started in 1908 in Jack County under the direction of Tom Marks. The girls part of the club started in 1912 in Milam County, headed by Edna Trigg, the first county home demonstration agent in Texas.

* * * * *

Buffalo bones picked up on the ranches around Odessa were sold to fertilizer factories for extra cash during the drought years. Carried to the nearest railhead, the bones sold for $20 a ton. The buffalo chips were burned for heat and for cooking.

* * * * *

The **All Valley Winter Vegetable Show**, held the first week in December in Pharr, is a wonderful display of the talents of the local 4-H and FFA clubs. Hundreds of varieties of vegetables are harvested, prepared, and shown by the members. After the awards are given and the auction is held for the Grand and Reserve Champion exhibits, the "Sack Sale" takes place. What is the "Sack Sale"? It is like a huge blue light special! For a set price the participants purchase a brown paper bag, line up, raise the bags over their head, and when the whistle is blown, a mad rush takes place as people fill their sacks with every vegetable imaginable.

* * * * *

When **Clara Barton**, the American Red Cross founder, came to the Pasadena area after the 1900 Galveston hurricane, she brought strawberry plants. Those strawberry plants started an industry that lasted for forty years. Pasadena has become an industrial town, and the strawberry fields are few, but the people of the area remember their past with an annual Strawberry Festival. The San Jacinto Day Foundation holds the festival on the weekend nearest April 21. Come celebrate with the world's largest strawberry shortcake.

* * * * *

Did you know that the **Lipan Indians** inhabited South Texas as late as 1906?

* * * * *

The first **Angora goats** were brought to Texas in 1853 by Colonel W.W. Haupt. George Kendall, a sheep rancher from 1857 to 1867, was one of the first to crossbreed the Mexican Churro sheep, a coarse wooled animal, with the Merino sheep which had fine wool. The Merino was brought to Texas by European immigrants. The land and climate of the Edwards Plateau area proved well suited and the sheep and goats flourished. Texas is the leading producer of sheep and goats in the nation, and the San Angelo area is the major market center for the animals and their wool.

* * * * *

San Saba is known as the "Pecan Capital of the World." Two to five million pounds of pecans are produced in this area each year. Pecans are native to this area and have been a cash crop since 1857. In the 1870s Edmond E. Risien came to the area from England. He found a light-colored, thin-shelled pecan which he named San Saba. He planted 600 trees using the nuts he found as seed. Many years later he cross-pollinated and selected certain nuts and qualities from this grove and gave the pecan industry many different varieties. It is upon this heritage that San Saba claims the title of Pecan Capital of the World.

* * * * *

Sonora has been called "The Capital of the Stockman's Paradise" because of its fine registered livestock. The Sutton County area is well known for its fine wool and mohair, and the Sonora Wool and Mohair Co. has one of the largest inland warehouses for the wool in the U.S.

* * * * *

The **Stratford Feedyard** was built in 1967 and feeds approximately 60,000 head of cattle at a time. Those cattle require 1.5 million pounds of feed—per day!

* * * * *

When **Coronado** left Mexico searching for the Seven Cities of Cibola in 1541, he took 500 head of cattle with him for food. These were possibly the first cattle in Texas. The missions became interested in raising the cattle. By 1716 Mission La Bahia del Espiritu Santo at Goliad had built up massive herds. Cattle identification came next with ear marks, numbers on the horns, and branding. The Spaniards had brought the horse to the New World, so it was only a matter of time before working the cattle on horseback came about. The missions and the favorable climate made the South Texas area a perfect place for the cattle industry to begin in Texas.

* * * * *

Rocksprings is the "Angora Goat Capital of the World" and home to the **American Angora Goat Breeders Association** since 1926.

* * * * *

The **first cattle ranch** established for the purpose of raising cattle as a business was established by empressario Don Martin de Leon in the area around Victoria. The ranch was approximately 30,000 acres. The brand, the connected letters E & J, was used by the de Leon family in Spain and by the Jesuit priests hundreds of years before. The brand, first recorded in Texas in 1807, stands for the "Espiritus de Jesus" or "Spirit of Jesus" and is believed to be the oldest in Texas in point of origin.

* * * * *

The missions raised cattle but this was not their sole enterprise. **Mission Espiritu Santo** is considered the first cattle ranch in Texas around 1770, with approximately 40,000 cattle. The Mission Rosario had around 30,000 head. The missions ranched in the area between the San Antonio River at Goliad and the Guadalupe at Victoria and had both branded and unbranded cattle on their ranches.

* * * * *

Some of the first **Brahman cattle** to enter the U.S. and Texas came in 1878 via a Dutch trading vessel through the port at Indianola.

* * * * *

It is estimated that over 10 million **longhorns** were driven north during a 30-year period after the Civil War. The cattle were only used for their hides in Texas, but driven north they were fattened on the midwestern grass for a waiting market.

* * * * *

Did you know that up to 92% of all **mohair** in the nation comes from West and Central Texas? That mohair comes from the town of Sonora and a 300-mile area around the town. This area also produces 40% of the total world production of mohair.

* * * * *

Bill Youngblood was killed by Indians outside of Weatherford in 1862. After his death, his friends found and killed the Indians, brought back Mr. Youngblood's scalp, and placed it on his head before he was buried.

* * * * *

The state of Texas opened the eastern section of Chambers County up to settlement in 1894. A **homestead grant** of 640 acres could be claimed by living on the grant for three years and paying $1200 in full or $50 per year interest until the original $1200 debt could be paid. A title and abstract was given when these two requirements were met.

* * * * *

The **Alabama-Coushatta Indian Reservation**, the oldest Indian reservation in Texas, is located in the Big Thicket between Livingston and Woodville. The reservation consists of 4600 acres close to the heart of the Big Thicket. Sam Houston was instrumental in creating the reservation in 1854 as a gift to the Indians for staying neutral during the Texas Revolution and actually helping Texans during the Runaway Scrape through East Texas.

* * * * *

Did you know that cattle and livestock **brands** and marks have to be recorded in the county clerk's office and must be renewed every ten years?

* * * * *

The Producer's Livestock Auction Co., in San Angelo, is the **largest sheep auction** in the nation and the second largest livestock auction in Texas. If you want to see for yourself, the sheep auction is held every Tuesday, and the cattle auction is held every Thursday.

* * * * *

The **Texas Rangers** were organized on the Colorado River, in what is now Colorado County, on August 5, 1823.

* * * * *

Mother Nature— Critters and Varmints

Texas longhorn—the breed is making a comeback with the desire for leaner beef.

The world's only **legally married pair of armadillos** live in Kountze, and on April 1 each year they celebrate Hoover and Starr's wedding anniversary. They were married in 1980. Perhaps they could let us in on their secret.

* * * * *

Ever see a **three-tusk elephant head**? The Hi-Plains Hospital has one on display along with other worldwide hunting trophies. The hospital is in Hale Center.

* * * * *

Gerry II is an elephant that lives at the Frank Buck Zoo in Gainesville. In 1981 a flood covered the zoo and many of the animals were lost, but Gerry II used her head and survived. She clung to a submerged tree and held her trunk above water for 24 hours until the raging waters subsided. No, this is not a Texas tale!

* * * * *

The Texas State Railroad, operated by the Texas Parks and Wildlife Department, runs antique steam engines along a 25.5 mile stretch between Rusk and Palestine—the **nation's longest and skinniest state park.**

* * * * *

The **Big Bend National Park**, established in 1944, consists of 1100 square miles, and the southern boundary of the park is 107 miles along the Rio Grande River.

* * * * *

There are more species of **cactus** in Texas than any other plant.

* * * * *

If you like **birding**, 3/4 of all American birds can be seen in Texas.

* * * * *

The "**Devil's Backbone**" is a winding ridge overlooking the Hill Country and is one of Texas' most scenic drives. Officially, the "Devil's Backbone" is R.M. 32.

* * * * *

Austin is known for a lot of things, but did you know it is the home to the **world's largest urban bat colony**? If you go to see the bats, try the Congress Ave. bridge on Town Lake. It is estimated that 750,000 Mexican free-tailed bats can be seen between April and October.

* * * * *

Jones State Forest, south of Conroe, is the nesting site of the rare **red-cockaded woodpecker**.

* * * * *

If you love walking in the woods, but don't know an oak tree from an elm, try the **Sylvan Nature Trail** southeast of Newton. The trail is a Texas Forestry Association Woodlands Trail with hiking paths about 1 1/4 miles long. Many species of forest trees along the trail are identified by signs.

* * * * *

If you know a fisherman that needs another whopper, take them to **Lake Walter B. Long**, east of Austin. They can fish for salt water flounder and redfish that have been stocked in the lake along with native freshwater species.

* * * * *

If you have never seen a **buffalo**, you may want to check out the private herd pastured eight miles east of Olney, across Highway 114 from the rest area. What a shock to our northern visitors!

* * * * *

Add to your collection of **sea shells** by visiting Mustang Island State Park and combing the five miles of Gulf beach frontage.

* * * * *

Texas is a great place to stay in winter, and the world's few remaining **whooping cranes** think so, too. The whooping cranes winter at the Aransas National Wildlife Refuge on a peninsula about 12 miles across the bay northeast of Rockport.

* * * * *

If you want to see **alligators**, look along the Brazos River in Wilderness Park, a 482-acre municipal park at Lake Jackson.

* * * * *

Over **1,100 types of plants** are found in Big Bend National Park.

* * * * *

The **Muleshoe National Wildlife Refuge**, in Muleshoe, is the oldest national wildlife refuge in Texas, founded in 1935. The flock of wintering sandhill cranes is the nation's largest.

* * * * *

Lake Sam Rayburn, located in the Angelina National Forest, is the largest body of water located totally within Texas. The lake covers 114,500 acres at normal capacity.

* * * * *

Falcon State Recreation Park, south of Zapata, has all of the normal facilities, plus one—a 3500 ft. airstrip!

* * * * *

If you like to fish, but can't take the Texas heat, Lake Texoma has several enclosed **fishing docks with air conditioning**.

* * * * *

You can fish for imported **peacock bass** at Coleto Creek Reservoir between Goliad and Victoria.

* * * * *

No hunting or shooting is permitted in a Texas state park; however, **hunting is allowed** in the four national forests, regulated by the Parks & Wildlife Department. Please check the rules and restrictions before planning a hunting trip.

* * * * *

The lower **Rio Grande Valley** area is the only place in the nation where white-fronted doves, chachalacas, and green jays can be seen.

* * * * *

The **Fairchild State Forest** was originally owned by the state prison system.

* * * * *

The best time to view wildlife in the **Aransas National Wildlife Refuge**, in Rockport, is November through March. This is when the greatest number of species can be seen.

* * * * *

Fort Griffin State Park is the home of the state maintained Texas **longhorn herd**.

* * * * *

The **Big Thicket National Preserve** was established by Congress in 1974.

* * * * *

The **Wild Basin Preserve** consists of 220 acres outside of Austin and is home to the endangered golden-cheeked warbler and the black-capped vireo.

* * * * *

Welder Wildlife Refuge, north of Sinton, is the largest privately endowed wildlife refuge in the world. Rancher Rob Welder provided for the refuge in his will.

* * * * *

The Dallas Zoo's reptile house has one of the world's largest **rattlesnake collections**.

* * * * *

Dinosaur Valley State Park in Glen Rose is on the Paluxy River, which flows over solid rock that contains the best preserved **dinosaur tracks** in Texas. The first sauropods tracks in the world were discovered here. Tracks of the duckbilled dinosaurs and the theropods have also been found in the area.

* * * * *

Fossil Rim Wildlife Ranch, in Glen Rose, consists of 2900 acres which are home to 30 rare and endangered species of African wildlife.

* * * * *

In Guadalupe Mountains National Park are four of the state's **highest mountain peaks**.

* * * * *

The **Galveston Island Beach** is 32 miles long.

* * * * *

Texas City Dike extends five miles into Galveston Bay with a 600-foot fishing pier beyond the tip of the dike. This pier has the deepest water for pier fishing in the state.

* * * * *

The state park within the city limits of Lubbock, **Mackenzie State Park**, draws more visitors than any other state park in Texas. The park is a day use facility only.

* * * * *

The **East Texas Piney Woods** area produces more than a million board feet of sawn timber annually.

* * * * *

Confederate Reunion Grounds State Park, near Mexia, was the reunion site for the Confederate States of America veterans from 1889 to 1946.

* * * * *

Chris Davidson Memorial Park in Midland is one of three parks in the U.S. that is **totally accessible to wheelchairs**.

* * * * *

The **McFaddin Refuge**, south of Port Arthur on the Gulf, contains one of the largest numbers of American alligators in Texas.

* * * * *

The **Natural Bridge Caverns** were discovered March 27, 1960, northwest of New Braunfels.

* * * * *

Even though the **Palo Duro Canyon** drops 1200 feet (plus or minus) from the rim to the canyon floor, you can drive to the floor of the canyon on paved roads.

* * * * *

Bastrop is one of the few remaining habitats for the **Houston toad**, an endangered species.

* * * * *

The Hill Country State Natural Area, in Bandera County, has about 5000 acres, **unrestricted equestrian trails**, and is the largest Texas state park open to horsemen.

* * * * *

Bandera is one of 13 counties in the state that have recorded **dinosaur tracks**.

* * * * *

The only native Texas game fish found exclusively within Texas is the **Guadalupe bass**.

* * * * *

There are more **waterfalls** in the Burnet area than anywhere else in Texas.

* * * * *

Burnet has the largest population of wintering **bald eagles** in Texas.

* * * * *

Longhorn Cavern, now in Longhorn Cavern State Park, is Texas' **oldest public cave**, and it is said to be the third largest cavern in the U.S. Dances and meetings were held in the cave during Prohibition. The cave was used to store gunpowder during the Civil War, and it was a hideout for Sam Bass the outlaw. The cavern is located outside Burnet.

* * * * *

Colorado Bend State Park is one of the most isolated parks in Texas—easier to reach by boat than by car! The park features primitive camping only. The park is south of Bend.

* * * * *

The **Monarch butterflies** make their last stop on Lake Sabine, near Bridge City, in October/November before their annual winter migration takes them across the Gulf of Mexico.

* * * * *

There are **52 varieties** of salt water fish in the offshore waters of the Gulf of Mexico.

* * * * *

The **whooping crane's** trip south takes 30 days and is 2500 miles long. It stays at Wood Buffalo National Park, Alberta, Canada in the summer and at Aransas National Wildlife Refuge from October through March.

* * * * *

The name El Rio de los Brazos de Dios (the River of the Arms of God) was shortened to Los Brazos de Dios. Later it was shortened again to Los Brazos, and today we know it as the **Brazos River**.

* * * * *

The **Palmetto State Park**, north of Gonzales, is used as a field laboratory by several Texas universities since the plant life is so abundant and most so rare.

* * * * *

The **National Zoo of Texas**, in Victoria, was selected by the U.S. Fish and Wildlife Service to participate in the red wolf species survival program, and in 1984 the first litter of near-extinct red wolf puppies was born.

* * * * *

If you like rabbits and want to see just about any kind there is, go to the annual **Rabbit Fest** in Copperas Cove in May. The four-day event has more than rabbits to enjoy, but breeders from around the country bring over 1000 rabbits of all kinds for the show and judging.

* * * * *

The Attwater Prairie Chicken National Wildlife Refuge was established north of Eagle Lake in 1972. The refuge is home to approximately 200 of the endangered birds—it is estimated that only 1400 of the birds still exist. This refuge is the only **Attwater's Prairie Chicken** refuge in the U.S.

* * * * *

The alligator caught in Eagle Lake in 1990—13 foot and 8 inches— is the **largest alligator on record** caught during the last 20 years in Texas.

* * * * *

The **Fort Worth Zoo** is the home of a rare white tiger and black rhino.

* * * * *

Did you know that the **Santa Ana National Wildlife Refuge** has 370 different types of birds inhabiting the 2080-acre refuge and 31 of these species are found nowhere else in the country?

* * * * *

Natural Bridge Caverns, located between San Antonio and New Braunfels, are named for the 60-foot natural limestone bridge that goes across its entrance. The caverns have been designated a Registered U.S. Natural Landmark.

* * * * *

Fort Hood, in Killeen, has over 190,000 acres that you can hunt on. All you need is a state hunting license and a Fort Hood permit.

* * * * *

The **official statewide eagle count** is held each year in January at Lake Buchanan.

* * * * *

Did you know that four of North America's five types of insect eating plants can be found in the **Big Thicket National Preserve**? The ones found are the pitcher plant, bladderwort, butterwort, and the sundew. The venus flytrap is the fifth type not found in the preserve.

* * * * *

The **Ellen Trout Zoo** started with a baby hippopotamus—a gag gift that Walter Trout received one Christmas from a friend. The baby hippo was given to the city, and the zoo grew from there with donations and contributions. The 10-acre zoo houses many endangered animals and is one of the only places to breed the Louisiana pine snake. The zoo is located in Lufkin.

* * * * *

The average depth of the **San Marcos River** in the Palmetto State Park area is only five feet. The lake in the park is only six feet in depth on average.

* * * * *

Mesquite trees, for the most part, are regarded as a problem. Once established, they spread their seeds and come up everywhere—the ranchers hate the tree. Mesquite is making a comeback today because the wood is an excellent barbecue wood, but the tree has been used in years past for many things. The wood of the mesquite tree is rot resistant, so it made long lasting fence posts for the farmers. Livestock eat the leaves, birds eat the beans, and humans eat the pods. Mesquite pods contain a lot of protein and are up to 40% sugar. Indians made the pods into flour, and early settlers used them to make jelly and wine. The Indians also used parts of the bark in making a cough syrup type medicine.

* * * * *

The Blechnum Occidentale, a tropical fern, is only found two places in the U.S., in the tropical regions of Florida and at **Enchanted Rock**. The basin bellflower and the rock quillwort are two other plants that only call Enchanted Rock home.

* * * * *

Llanite is a mineral that is found only in Llano County. This mineral is found nowhere else in the world. Llanite is a rare type of brown granite with sky blue crystals and rusty-pink feldspar. The largest piece of polished llanite in the world is on display at the Badu House, an historic inn in Llano.

* * * * *

More than five million **buffalo** were killed in the Southwest in one year—from 1872 to 1873! The slaughter in the Panhandle of Texas numbered 100,000 from 1877 to 1878.

* * * * *

Although there are only four seasons in a year, the Big Bend and Davis Mountain region have what they call their **"fifth season,"** around September and October. Just after the rainy period, the area experiences another "spring" with everything covered in blooms.

* * * * *

125

Did you know that the **Rio Grande beaver** digs burrows into the river banks instead of building lodges?

* * * * *

The **Big Bend mosquitofish** live in the smallest habitat of any known vertebrate—a 1/2 acre pond near Rio Grande Village. At one time there were only two males and one female left in the world.

* * * * *

When the state of Texas purchased the 264,000-acre area now known as the **Big Bend Ranch State Natural Area,** the amount of public land owned by the state doubled. This area has a history of violent volcanic eruptions. The volcanoes date back to 28 to 44 million years ago. Some of the violent eruptions blew out between 100 to 300 cubic kilometers of rock, ash, and lava. The 1980 Mount St. Helens eruption ejected only one cubic kilometer of debris.

* * * * *

Sabal Palm Sanctuary is an Audubon sanctuary covering 172 acres southeast of Brownsville. The **sabal palm** is the only palm native to extreme South Texas.

* * * * *

One of Aransas County's unique birds is the **black-bellied tree duck** which whistles instead of quacking and has claws on the end of its webbed feet. Their claws allow them to land and stay in trees.

* * * * *

In the winter of 1991 the **whooping crane** population numbered 132 compared to only 15 in 1941. The bird stands five feet tall with a wing span of 7.5 feet. The Aransas National Wildlife Refuge is the whooping crane's winter home.

* * * * *

The **San Antonio Zoo** is the only zoo to have a whooping crane pair.

* * * * *

The **concho pearl** is a natural pearl produced by mussels found in the San Angelo, Concho River area. A quality pearl only happens once in every 100 mussels. The concho pearls are found in the colors of pink, lavender, and purple and are more rare than pearls found in saltwater mussels. The pearls start with the intrusion of a microscopic parasite into the mussel, not a grain of sand or some other foreign object. Because of a destructive "pearl rush" during the period of 1979 to 1982, an old 1910 law, requiring a license to harvest mussels in Texas, was revived.

* * * * *

Only four zoos in the United States have **koalas**—and the San Antonio Zoo is one of them!

* * * * *

Buescher State Park, close to Smithville, is part of the **Lost Pines of Texas Forest**.

* * * * *

Laguna Atascosa National Wildlife Refuge is on the lower portion of the Gulf Coast of Texas, near **Rio Hondo**. The refuge is the nation's southernmost water fowl refuge.

* * * * *

Did you know that less than 5% of the natural habitat remains in the **Lower Rio Grande Valley**?

* * * * *

Before the **buffalo** were hunted, there were approximately 60 to 75 million head. Around 1830, 40 million head still existed, but by 1883 less than one thousand buffalo were left in the country.

* * * * *

The **National Fish Hatchery** is located in Uvalde and operated by the U.S. Fish and Wildlife Service. The hatchery produces and distributes 2.5 million fish per year all over the nation.

* * * * *

Texas has ten different **habitats** in the state and 700 species of animals are found within her boundaries. From marshes to desert, Texas offers a wide range of climates for these many different kinds of animals.

* * * * *

The **Texas Zoo**, in Victoria, was established in 1976, and in 1984 it was proclaimed by the Legislature to be the "National Zoo of Texas." The zoo consists only of Texas species and has over 200 mammals, birds, reptiles, amphibians, and fish. The zoo also houses the endangered species of red wolf, ocelot, bald eagle, margay, jaguarundi, coati, and black bear, found only in far West Texas.

* * * * *

In 1829, 350 men and boys from around Parker County gathered to shoot the rabbits that were destroying the watermelon crops around

Millsap. Probably one of the largest rabbit hunts organized in Texas.

* * * * *

The **Big Thicket** once contained 3.5 million acres and is now less than 300,000. Of this figure, only 84,550 acres are protected in the Big Thicket National Preserve.

* * * * *

The Big Thicket National Preserve, established in 1974, was designated an **International Biosphere Reserve** in 1981 by the United Nations. This protected area will provide a standard for measuring human impact on the environment.

* * * * *

Special licenses and tags are required if you want to go **alligator hunting**. If you want to trap fur bearing animals in Texas, this requires a trapper's license.

* * * * *

The GCCA/CPL Marine Development Center at Corpus Christi, completed in 1982, is the world's first and only **saltwater redfish** production hatchery. This hatchery produces an average of 15-20 million redfish, or red drum, fingerlings per year that are released in the bays and the Gulf of Mexico. You can tour the facility.

* * * * *

Chapter 7 ————————————

Simply Trivia

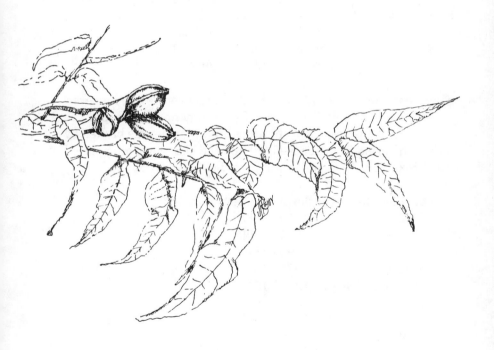

Pecans still in the husk. The pecan is the state tree and was officially adopted in 1919.

State Name:	From the Indian word Tejas, meaning friends
State Motto:	Friendship, officially adopted 1930
State Nickname:	Lone Star State
State Bird:	Mockingbird, officially adopted 1927
State Tree:	Pecan, officially adopted 1919
State Flower:	Bluebonnet, officially adopted 1901
State Gem:	Topaz, officially adopted 1969
State Food:	Chili, officially adopted 1977
State Shell:	Lightning Whelk, officially adopted 1987
State Fish:	Guadalupe bass, officially adopted 1989
State Stone:	Petrified palmwood, officially adopted 1969
State Grass:	Sideoats Gramma, officially adopted 1971
State Song:	"Texas, Our Texas," officially adopted 1929
State Folk Dance:	The square dance, officially adopted 1991
State Holidays:	Texas Independence Day, March 2
	San Jacinto Day, April 21
	Emancipation Day, June 19
	LBJ's Birthday, August 27

* * * * *

There have been six different **flags** flown over Texas, however, there have been eight changes of government—Spain and the U.S. ruled Texas two separate times. Spain's rule was broken by a French period from 1685—1690 and the U.S. governing period was broken by the Confederate period of 1861 - 1865.

The flags that have flown over Texas:

Spain	1519 - 1685
France	1685 - 1690
Spain	1690 - 1821
Mexico	1821 - 1836
Republic of Texas	1836 - 1845
United States	1845 - 1861
Confederacy	1861 - 1865
United States	1865 - present

* * * * *

If you take the first letter of the street names that connect Main St. in **Fredericksburg**, they spell WELCOME going east and COME BACK going west.

* * * * *

Did you know that **Round Top** has the lowest property tax rate in Texas, and it has been the same since 1877?!!!!!! For your information, Round Top's charter was approved in 1877. Think we ought to send these guys to Washington? Obviously they know how to handle a budget!

* * * * *

According to the Upshur County Historical Commission, there are three **Confederate graves** in the Mt. Gilead Cemetery with markers that have curved, almost pointed tops. The Union markers are flat on top. The design for the Confederate markers was chosen to "discourage some Damn Yankee from sitting atop one of the stones. It was their desire to give him a 'Pain in the Ass' if he did so." Their words, not mine.

* * * * *

The **Fifty Cent Act** was passed on July 14, 1879. The act allowed public lands to be sold at 50 cents per acre to pay public debt and establish a permanent school fund. In 1994 we are still trying to establish a fair way to fund our schools—wonder if the 50-cents-per-acre offer still stands?!

* * * * *

The **"Old Three Hundred,"** the first families brought to Texas to colonize the area under legal contract with the government of Mexico by Stephen F. Austin, only numbered 297 families.

* * * * *

It took 50 ox-drawn wagons to bring the **archives** and furniture of the Texas government to the new capital in Austin from Houston around the first of September 1839.

* * * * *

On March 26, 1918, Governor W.P. Hobby signed a bill giving women the **right to vote** in primary elections and in all nominating conventions.

* * * * *

Although most Texans recognize the **Battle at Gonzales**, over the cannon, on October 2, 1935, as the first trouble with Mexico, the Battle of Velasco on June 26, 1832 was probably the first bloodshed between Texas and Mexico.

* * * * *

The **Guerrero Decree** of September 15, 1829 abolished slavery in the Republic of Mexico, which Texas was a part of at the time.

* * * * *

In 1850 the Texas Legislature passed a law requiring that all county seats be located within five miles of the **geographic center** of each county.

* * * * *

The only Olympic-size ice arena in the state is the North Texas Ice Arena in **Irving**.

* * * * *

There are five Texas streams named **Salado**.

* * * * *

Architect **Wesley Clarke Dobson**, of Waco, designed ten Texas courthouses.

* * * * *

Texas A&M University, established in 1876, was the state's first public institution of higher education and Texas' **first land-grant college**.

* * * * *

If you are tired of the library being closed when you need information, try the local library in **Chappell Hill**. The library, organized in 1893, is a self-service facility and the patrons have individual keys!

* * * * *

Arnim & Lane Mercantile is a genuine country store in **Flatonia** that has been in operation since 1886. The store offers antique as well as modern merchandise.

* * * * *

Dimmitt has the only corn-wet milling plant in Texas—or the Southwest. The American Fructose plant produces fructose corn syrup, dry starch, and livestock feed. You can take a tour of the plant in operation.

* * * * *

El Dorado Woolens, in El Dorado, is the only woolen mill in the Southwest weaving fabrics from wool and mohair produced on West Texas ranches.

* * * * *

In 1882 the state of Texas traded 3,050,000 acres of land to a Chicago corporation for construction of the state capitol. The three million acres became the **XIT Ranch** operated by a London company.

* * * * *

Calvert had the largest cotton gin in the world—in 1871, that is.

* * * * *

The **San Jacinto Monument** is 15 feet taller than the Washington Monument. The star that tops the monument is 35 feet high and weighs 220 tons.

* * * * *

The **Governor's Mansion** was built in 1856. The governors and their families live in a private second floor apartment. The other areas of the mansion are open for public tours.

* * * * *

The **National Wildflower Research Center** was established in 1982 on 60 acres east of Austin on land donated by Lady Bird Johnson. You can come here from all parts of the country and receive information on plants that are native to the region or state that you are interested in.

* * * * *

The **State Capitol complex** is on 46 acres.

* * * * *

The **San Marcos River** has over 200 springs.

* * * * *

The **State Fair of Texas** consists of 200 acres.

* * * * *

The **Fort Worth Convention Center** spans an area of 14 downtown blocks.

* * * * *

During the Civil War, a pistol factory in **Lancaster** produced the Colt .44 Dragoon revolver that collectors call the "Tucke & Sherrod Confederate Colt."

* * * * *

Bishop's Palace, located in Galveston, is the state's only structure on the list of the nation's 100 outstanding buildings by the American Institute of Architects.

* * * * *

There are 5100 square miles of lakes and streams in Texas. Texas is second only to Alaska in volume of **inland water**.

* * * * *

The first outhouse in the state to receive a historical marker, the **Arnold Outhouse,** is located in Henderson and was erected for a local attorney in 1908. The restored "three-holer" can be seen at the Depot Museum and Children's Discovery Center.

* * * * *

The city of Laredo has been governed under seven flags—one more than the state of Texas. Laredo served as the capital of the unsuccessful **Republic of the Rio Grande**—1839 to 1841.

* * * * *

La Porte is the home of the **Houston Yacht Club**, the second oldest yacht club in the U.S.

* * * * *

Tehuacana Hills is the highest point between Houston and Dallas, in Mexia.

* * * * *

The **Y.O. Ranch**, west of Mountain Home, has more blackbuck than are in their native land of India.

* * * * *

The *Quitman Daily News* was published in 1873 by **James Stephen Hogg**.

* * * * *

The first **farmer's grange** in Texas was established in Salado in 1873.

* * * * *

The **Ellis County courthouse** clock's bell striker exceeds 800 pounds.

* * * * *

In 1885 the **Leon County courthouse** in Centerville burned, and a new courthouse was completed in 1887. The new building was built of slate bricks that were handmade near the site of the new courthouse. The slate brick courthouse is one of the oldest in Texas of this type construction.

* * * * *

The **adobe courthouse** in Sierra Blanca is the Southwest's only governmental structure of adobe still in use.

* * * * *

The Red River County courthouse in Clarksville was built in 1885 and included a clock tower. The clock was called **"Old Red"** and continued to operate until 1961 when it was converted to electricity. The clock went a little crazy soon after that, striking 120 times before someone unplugged it!

* * * * *

A **Zero Stone** is located on the courthouse square of Fort Stockton. The stone was placed by a survey crew in 1859 and was used as the origin point for all land surveys in this part of West Texas.

* * * * *

The **first court** of the Third Judicial District of the Republic of Texas convened in 1837 under a live oak tree in Columbus. Today, a historical marker identifies the spot.

* * * * *

Forest lands in Texas are estimated to be 23.4 million acres.

* * * * *

Ninety-one **mountains** in Texas are more than a mile high.

* * * * *

Texas has a 624-mile **coastline**.

* * * * *

Lake Livingston, an 82,600-acre reservoir on the Trinity River, is located in four counties.

* * * * *

The Texas coastline, along the Gulf of Mexico, contains more than 600 historic **shipwrecks**.

* * * * *

The 1850 census recorded 213,000 people in Texas. The 1980 **census** showed a slight growth—14 million!

* * * * *

Guadalupe Peak is the tallest point in Texas—8751 feet high.

* * * * *

Big Bend National Park encompasses 801,163 acres.

* * * * *

Texas is the **second largest state** in area. Alaska is first. Texas is also the second largest state when it comes to inland water— Alaska is number one again.

* * * * *

Big Bend National Park has more than 160 miles of paved roads and 256 miles of dirt roads.

* * * * *

There are more than 1000 state maintained **rest stops** in Texas and these account for about an eighth of all the rest stops in the nation.

* * * * *

Port of Corpus Christi is the sixth busiest port in the nation.

* * * * *

The **first telephone line** in Texas was established in Galveston on March 18, 1878 by A.H. Belo.

* * * * *

Lake Granite Shoals was renamed on April 22, 1965 to Lake Lyndon B. Johnson. Most of us know it as **Lake LBJ**.

* * * * *

The **Daughters of the Republic of Texas** formed November 6, 1891.

* * * * *

The **Texas Bar Association** was permanently organized at Galveston on December 12, 1882.

* * * * *

In 1929 only five people filed **income tax returns** in Andrews County.

* * * * *

Andrews County has one of the lowest property tax rates in the nation.

* * * * *

The only **Texas Revolution soldier** buried in Tarrant County is William M. Rice, buried in Ash Creek Cemetery in Azle.

* * * * *

Did you know that **Six Flags Over Texas** in Arlington was created by Disneyland designer Randall Duell? In the late 1950s Angus G. Wynne, Jr., the son of a wealthy oilman, brought Mr. Duell in to create a theme park that would be full of fantasy yet easier to get to and more affordable for family entertainment. Six Flags opened in 1961, and Wynne built six more Six Flags parks in other areas of the U.S.

* * * * *

When the Lucas Well at **Spindletop** blew in, oil shot 200 feet into the air. An estimated 800,000 barrels of oil were lost before the well was capped nine days later.

* * * * *

The **Bastrop Chamber of Commerce** has its offices in the 1890 Old Iron Front Saloon.

* * * * *

Three men from **Bastrop** signed the Texas Declaration of Independence, 11 died at the Alamo, and 60 fought in the Battle of San Jacinto.

* * * * *

Did you know that only 14 homes have been constructed in the last five years in **Ballinger**? Wonder why, since the average cost of a lot is $2250.00.

* * * * *

Did you know that **Hank Williams'** signature is still on one of the tables at Arkey Blue's Silver Dollar in Bandera County?

* * * * *

There are no railroads in **Bandera County**. That is truly amazing considering the large part that the railroads played in the development of Texas.

* * * * *

The Charles Fagan collection at the **Frontier Times Museum** in Bandera includes two shrunken heads.

* * * * *

John Tumlinson was the first Texas Ranger killed in the line of duty on July 6, 1823, by the Indians. Sixteen of Tumlinson's descendants have served the Rangers.

* * * * *

Stephen F. Austin colonized the **Clear Lake** area in 1825, selling the land for 12 1/2 cents an acre.

* * * * *

In 1927 the *Houston Post-Dispatch* offered lots in **Clear Lake Shores** for $69.50 with a six-month subscription!

* * * * *

Originally, there were 23 **counties** in Texas—we now have 254.

* * * * *

Did you know the flag flown at half-mast over the **Treue Der Union** monument in Comfort is a 36-star flag, used by the U.S. at the time of the Civil War?

* * * * *

President Lyndon B. Johnson received his first teaching position in **Cotulla**.

* * * * *

If you get sick and need a doctor, **Victoria** is where you need to be. Did you know that Victoria has the highest number of family doctors per capita in Texas, and it ranks sixth in the nation?

* * * * *

Did you know that **Fort Hood** is the state's largest employer? The payroll of Fort Hood is around 67 million dollars—per month!

* * * * *

Did you know that the sign over Judge Roy Bean's establishment, **The Jersey Lily**, was actually misspelled by a sign painter—it should have been "The Jersey Lilly." The sign has never been corrected.

* * * * *

The first movie location built in Texas, **Alamo Village**, is located seven miles north of Brackettville. It is an exact replica of the Alamo with a complete town to look like San Antonio in the 1800s, built for John Wayne's movie *The Alamo*. Construction started in September 1957, and filming started in August of 1959. It took over one million handmade adobe bricks to make the village buildings. The village was also the location for the filming of *Lonesome Dove*.

* * * * *

Dallas has more than 830 shopping centers and more retail space per capita than any other city in the U.S.

* * * * *

There are 40 lakes and reservoirs within 100 miles of the center of **Dallas**.

* * * * *

There is a two-mile **underground tunnel system** in Dallas that connects major downtown buildings, shops, and restaurants.

* * * * *

It is estimated that it would take over five years to eat at every **Dallas** restaurant—that is if you ate at a different place three times a day!

* * * * *

Translated from Latin, **Corpus Christi** means "body of Christ." The city received its name in 1519 when Alonzo de Pineda discovered the area on the Catholic holy day Feast of Corpus Christi.

* * * * *

Lake Texoma has 600 miles of shoreline and is the tenth largest lake in the country.

* * * * *

In 1890 the University of North Texas was founded as **Texas Normal College** in Denton.

* * * * *

The high school in **Denver City** was built in 1940. It was the first brick building in town.

* * * * *

The only **tannery** in Moore County is in Dumas. Did you know that they process 3500 hides per day?

* * * * *

In 1890 there were only 15 people in **Moore County**, according to the federal census of the time.

* * * * *

The **Bi-State Justice Center** in Texarkana is the only two-state law enforcement and legal facility in the country.

* * * * *

The Admiral Nimitz State Historical Park, in Fredericksburg, contains a **Japanese Garden of Peace** behind the Steamboat Hotel structure, a gift from the people of Japan.

* * * * *

In 1949 the **Waco Air Force Base** was renamed Connally AFB, and in 1950 it became known as the James T. Connally AFB. This was the only base in the U.S. that used a first name.

* * * * *

The first business in **Temple** was a saloon.

* * * * *

In 1927 the police siren in **Borger** went off at 9:00 p.m. to warn the children it was time to go home.

* * * * *

Did you know that it is illegal to dig for **arrowheads**? Just hope you find one on top of the ground!

* * * * *

Brownfield became the county seat of Terry County on June 28, 1904, by a five-vote margin over the village of Gomez.

* * * * *

Baylor University was founded at **Independence**, Washington County, in 1846 and later moved to Waco in 1886.

* * * * *

The Kenneth Medlock Memorial Range at Brady Lake has been the headquarters for the **Texas Muzzle Loaders** for the last 20 years. Yes, they do wear coonskin caps and buckskins!

* * * * *

When the State Legislature created **Brown County** in 1856, only two families lived in the county. At the time, they had been in the area less than two months.

* * * * *

Seawolf Park on Pelican Island was once an immigrant quarantine station.

* * * * *

Out back of the Coryell County Historical Museum in Gatesville is the **old log jail** built in 1855—the first building built by Coryell County. The jail was only big enough for the guard; the prisoner was kept underground and fed through a trap door in

the floor. Don't think there were very many jail breaks—what do
you think?!

* * * * *

The Coryell County courthouse's interior dome features a colorful **Texas star-patterned stained glass dome**. The
courthouse itself was built in 1897 of hand-cut stone quarried
across the Leon River.

* * * * *

On September 9 and 10, 1921, **Thrall**, in Williamson County,
received 38 inches of rain in 24 hours. At the time, this was a
record rainfall in the U.S.

* * * * *

According to one story I heard, the first jail in **Williamson
County** was a wagon turned upside down to hold the prisoner
in place—yes, that probably would do it!

* * * * *

The First Presbyterian Church in **Georgetown** still rings the
bell that was purchased in 1877 for the church.

* * * * *

The **Gonzales courthouse** is in the form of a Greek cross.

* * * * *

In the 1980 census, 34% of the population of **Giddings** claimed
German ancestry. This largely German community draws its
heritage from the many German immigrants of the 1870 to 1890
period. The settlers were mainly Wendish Lutherans, and
Giddings publishes the only Wendish type newspaper, the
Giddings Deutches Volksblatt.

* * * * *

Did you know that in 1990, 46,545 tons (yes, tons) of sugar and
molasses was shipped through the **Port of Harlingen**?

* * * * *

Did you know that in 1983 **Robertson County** had 10 attorneys
and one jail that would hold 14?

* * * * *

The **Weslaco water tower** is now used as a theatre. The water
works were founded in 1920 and the tank was built in 1929.

* * * * *

Did you know that during the 1800s, you would get a much stiffer sentence for **stealing a horse** than for killing a man?!

* * * * *

The **first woman inmate** in Huntsville was convicted in 1854.

* * * * *

In 1935 twenty **executions** were carried out—the largest number in one year.

* * * * *

Spur 94 in **Huntsville**, "Sam Houston Memorial Drive," is Texas' shortest highway.

* * * * *

There are more than 334 parks in **Houston**.

* * * * *

Iraan is the birthplace of **Alley Oop**, the cartoon strip, born in 1927. Since 1965, Iraan has celebrated a biannual Alley Oop Day celebration.

* * * * *

The original map for the to-be city of **Irving** was drawn on a 6- x 13-foot tablecloth.

* * * * *

The first courthouse in **Kaufman** was a remodeled blacksmith shop.

* * * * *

Keller was called Athol. The streets that were named on the original 40-acre town site have retained their 1881 names.

* * * * *

The **Rocks & Minerals Land Area** consists of McCulloch, San Saba, Menard, Mason, Llano, Sutton, and Kimble counties. This area in the Hill Country of Texas is great for rock hounds and rock climbers.

* * * * *

At one time **Kilgore** had 1200 oil derricks. In the 1940s the wells inside the city limits could supply the nation's petroleum needs at full production.

* * * * *

The **Naval Air Station Kingsville**, in Kingsville, graduates approximately 200 naval aviators per year.

* * * * *

The Llano jail, built in 1895 with Llano County granite, was referred to by inmates as "**Red Top**" because of its red roof. The gallows are still in place on the third and fourth floors.

* * * * *

Did you know that master stone cutters were brought to Texas from Scotland to complete the **State Capitol** building?

* * * * *

The **Gregg County Airport**, in Longview, has been designated an alternate landing site for the space shuttle.

* * * * *

The last job that the **Dalton Gang** pulled was the Longview bank robbery in 1894.

* * * * *

On average, 12,000 cars and trucks cross the border into the U.S. from Mexico through Nuevo Laredo to **Laredo** each day.

* * * * *

Did you know that **topaz**, the official state gem of Texas, is only found in one area of Texas—Mason County? Usually found in streambeds or creeks, topaz occurs in granite outcroppings and can sometimes be found on top of the ground. What is the prettiest topaz? Even though topaz can also be found in clear, brown, and yellow, the sky blue stones are thought by some to be the most beautiful, cut in what else but the Lone Star cut!

* * * * *

Another name for hanging was **rope poisoning**!

* * * * *

The site where **Mercedes** was built was known as the "Pear Orchard." Not because of pears, but because of prickly pear cactus!

* * * * *

Did you know that **McKinney** is located the same distance from Dallas, Denton, Sherman, and Greenville? What is unusual about this is that all of these towns are the county seats of the surrounding counties!

* * * * *

In 1849 the average taxable value of land in **Collin County** was 68 cents per acre.

* * * * *

In 1870 two **meteorites** were found about eight miles west of McKinney, the largest being over 200 pounds. The Peabody Museum at Harvard has a piece, the Field Museum of Natural History in Chicago has another, and still other pieces are all over the world—except none can be found in McKinney!

* * * * *

Fifteen counties have been named for men who once lived in **Marshall**.

* * * * *

The Hochwald House in Marshall was built around 1895. The house has an **automobile turn-table** in the driveway! It is believed to be the only one in Texas.

* * * * *

The first **library** in Marshall opened in 1900 in a feed store loft with hay bales for chairs and 174 books in stock. One year later the library moved to the City Hall where annual reading tickets were sold for $1. The funds from the reading tickets and money raised by the area civic and library clubs provided 69 years of service without the use of public tax revenues.

* * * * *

McAllen has an interesting way of naming its streets. Coming from the north, the east-west avenues are named for trees in alphabetical order (except there is not a street that begins with a Z since they did not know of a 'Z' tree), then flowers, and then birds—all in alphabetical order.

* * * * *

Did you know that **Dinero** got its name because Santa Anna's soldiers buried their gold in this location as they were fleeing after the defeat at San Jacinto?

* * * * *

The **tourist industry** is second to agriculture as the Rio Grande Valley's source of income. There are over 500 RV and mobile home parks in the five-county area along the border. Many people from all over the country and Canada come to the area and stay the winter. $200 million dollars in tourist industry revenue was brought in during the winter of 1988—1989 in the Valley area.

*****

Bull fights in Texas? In Nacogdoches, close to where the First Presbyterian Church now stands, was the bull ring where fights were held in Spanish days.

*****

Ector County will never have the chance to relocate its courthouse without losing its courthouse square. You see, back in 1891 a gentleman donated the courthouse square to the county with the provision that the land could never be sold or the courthouse moved—otherwise they lose ownership.

*****

The **Permian Basin** had 25,000 producing oil wells by 1952.

*****

The earliest known discovery of the **Odessa Meteor Crater** was made in 1892 by Julius Henderson. Estimated time of the fall was 20,000 years ago with the largest depression being about 550 feet in diameter and 100 feet in depth, when it was newly formed. Smaller craters were also in the vicinity of this main crater. For many years the hole was referred to as a "blowout" until the 1920s when D. Moreau Barringer and Dr. E.H. Sellards recognized the depression as a meteor crater. The '30s and '40s saw extensive excavations and scientific studies done by Dr. Sellards and Glen Evans. World War II ended the studies.

*****

During the depression there was a shortage of police officers in the **Pharr** community. The City Hall installed an electric light on top of the building to alert officers when there was trouble.

*****

The **shrimp season** in the Gulf of Mexico is seven months long.

*****

The population of the **Rio Grande Valley** is around 700,000—until another 250,000 winter Texans come to visit and stay for a while.

*****

Port Lavaca Lighthouse Beach and Bird Sanctuary, or **Lighthouse Beach** for short, has the only natural sand beach in the area.

*****

There is a **shipwreck** in north Lavaca Bay believed to be one of LaSalle's ships.

$$* * * * *$$

Did you know that Lorimar Television owns the trademark name rights to the **Southfork Ranch**? The actual property made famous as the Southfork Ranch can't be called by that name. The new owners of the property, 41 acres and the mansion, purchased it for $42.6 million in 1992. By the way, did you know the mansion has 5,931 square feet—heated and cooled I presume!

$$* * * * *$$

The Sacred Heart Catholic Church in **Rowlett** was built in 1899 facing the railroad track. In 1922 the parishioners decided to turn the church around to face the new Bankhead Highway, now Main Street, which they did and reset it on the original foundation. The eight stained glass windows in the church were imported from Germany.

$$* * * * *$$

In 1990 the population of **Rowlett** was over 23,000, but there were only 39 people living there 85 years old or older.

$$* * * * *$$

As Texans we often encounter **hurricanes**, but do you know the difference between a tropical storm and a hurricane? A tropical storm has distinct circular motion with sustained wind speeds of 39 to 73 miles per hour. A hurricane is a tropical cyclone with sustained wind speeds of 74 plus miles per hour. Anything with speeds of 38 miles per hour or less turning in a circular motion at the surface of the water is termed a tropical depression. All of these storms start on the water and move inland.

$$* * * * *$$

The Legislature made **square dancing** the official Texas folk dance in 1991.

$$* * * * *$$

The Confederate soldier statue in **Rusk** faces south. What is so unusual about that? Most Confederate soldier statues in the South face north to "send the Yankees home."

$$* * * * *$$

The **Texas Railroad Commission** was established to enforce state antitrust laws and promote fair business practices. The commission was established during James Hogg's administration in 1891.

* * * * *

Did you know that there are over 10,000 official Texas **historical markers** throughout Texas?

* * * * *

Average rainfall of **San Saba County** is 28.22 inches per year. During the drought of 1953 to 1956, a total of 63.08 inches of rain was recorded, and 10.12 inches of this occurred during the months of May and June 1955.

* * * * *

At the **Battle of San Jacinto**, the Mexicans lost 630 men, the Texans lost only 9.

* * * * *

The **Alamo Mission** buildings remained in ruins after the battle in 1836, until 1849. In 1849 the U.S. Army repaired the buildings and added the upper portion of the facade that distinguishes the Alamo today.

* * * * *

Theodore Roosevelt's horse "Texas," ridden in the charge of San Juan Hill in the Spanish American War, was given to him by his cousin, Colonel Moore of **Seguin**.

* * * * *

In 1989 **Gains County** was number one in oil production, cotton production, and in peanut production in Texas.

* * * * *

The Haynes Mattress Factory opened in **Sealy** in 1885. Its owner, Daniel Haynes, invented the machines and the process for manufacturing a felted cotton, nontufted mattress. In 1889 Haynes sold the rights to his mattress materials and manufacturing process all over the South, but not his name. The Haynes Mattress was termed the Sealy Mattress by the public since it was made in Sealy. The trade name, Sealy Mattress, was adopted by the Sealy Mattress Co. after it purchased the Haynes patents and equipment in 1906 and moved to Dallas. The Haynes Mattress Factory was officially re-established in Sealy in 1909 by Haynes and his son. The business finally closed in 1975 after several ownership changes.

* * * * *

The University of Texas **M.D. Anderson Cancer Center** Science Park Research Division is located adjacent to Buescher State Park, two miles from Smithville. It is here that 49 doctoral level scientists study the cause and prevention of cancer. The research center has 150 employees.

* * * * *

In November 1894 half of the town of **Shiner** burned. The fire was started by an explosion set off when burglars blew open a safe in a local store.

* * * * *

There are 16 lighthouses along the Texas coast, but the **Port Isabel Lighthouse** is the only one open to the public.

* * * * *

South Padre Island was separated from Padre Island in 1964 when the **Port of Mansfield Gulf Channel** was complete, dividing the island in two.

* * * * *

Tourism is the only industry on South Padre Island.

* * * * *

The state leased **convicts** to farms for labor until 1836. At that time the lease system was abolished and the Legislature told the Penitentiary Board to buy land and work the convicts themselves.

* * * * *

Texarkana, Texas is 21 square miles in Bowie County, and Texarkana, Arkansas is 16.5 square miles in Miller County.

* * * * *

Did you know that "**Popeye**" was created by the cartoonist E.C. Segar in 1919 in Victoria?

* * * * *

Ozona is the only town in Crockett County, a county with approximately 2800 square miles.

* * * * *

Ingram was once known as "America's only all-rock city" because most of the town's buildings were made of native stone. The area known as the "old Ingram Loop" made up of old stone buildings now filled with shops and arts and crafts for visitors.

* * * * *

The Colorado County courthouse in **Columbus** has a Tiffany glass dome in the District Court room.

* * * * *

Did you know that 20% of all Texas buildings on the National Register of Historic Places are located in **Waxahachie**?

* * * * *

The **Ellis County jail**, built in 1888, did have a revolving "squirrel-cage" cell. The revolving cell has been removed.

* * * * *

Waxahachie's early street paving was out of wood blocks instead of bricks to quiet the noise of the wagon wheels and horses hooves.

* * * * *

The **Ellis County courthouse** was constructed so that each of the four doors face directly in a compass direction—north, south, east, and west. There is a tale that the courthouse was supposed to have been designed after Solomon's Temple.

* * * * *

Did you know the **Parker County courthouse**, built after the 1884 fire which destroyed the existing courthouse, cost $55,555.55?

* * * * *

The **falls** that gave Wichita Falls its name washed away in a flood over 100 years ago, but in 1986 a 54-foot man-made waterfall was built to replace the original falls. The water flow is 35 to 45 feet wide, and a pump recirculates 3500 gallons of water per minute.

* * * * *

Tyler County is more than 90% wooded.

* * * * *

The **Texas Scottish Rite Hospital** for children, in Dallas, provided treatment for over 10,000 children in 1990—at no charge.

* * * * *

Texas has **254 counties**. The following is a list of those counties, their county seats, the years they were created and the population according to the 1990 census:

County	County Seat	Year Created	Population
Anderson	Palestine	1846	48,024
Andrews	Andrews	1876	14,338
Angelina	Lufkin	1846	69,884
Aransas	Rockport	1871	17,892
Archer	Archer City	1858	7,973
Armstrong	Claude	1876	2,021
Atascosa	Jourdanton	1856	30,533
Austin	Bellville	1837	19,832
Bailey	Muleshoe	1876	7,064
Bandera	Bandera	1856	10,562
Bastrop	Bastrop	1836	38,263
Baylor	Seymour	1858	4,385
Bee	Beeville	1857	25,135
Bell	Belton	1850	191,088
Bexar	San Antonio	1836	1,185,394
Blanco	Johnson City	1858	5,972
Borden	Gail	1876	799
Bosque	Meridian	1854	15,125
Bowie	Boston	1840	81,665
Brazoria	Angleton	1836	191,707
Brazos	Bryan	1841	121,862
Brewster	Alpine	1887	8,681
Briscoe	Silverton	1876	1,971
Brooks	Falfurrias	1911	8,204
Brown	Brownwood	1856	34,371
Burleson	Caldwell	1846	13,625
Burnet	Burnet	1852	22,677
Caldwell	Lockhart	1848	26,392
Calhoun	Port Lavaca	1846	19,053
Callahan	Baird	1858	11,859
Cameron	Brownsville	1848	260,120
Camp	Pittsburg	1874	9,904
Carson	Panhandle	1876	6,576
Cass	Linden	1846	29,982
Castro	Dimmitt	1876	9,070
Chambers	Anahuac	1858	20,088
Cherokee	Rusk	1846	41,049
Childress	Childress	1876	5,953
Clay	Henrietta	1857	10,024
Cochran	Morton	1876	4,377

County	County Seat	Year Created	Population
Coke	Robert Lee	1889	3,424
Coleman	Coleman	1858	9,710
Collin	McKinney	1846	264,036
Collingsworth	Wellington	1876	3,573
Colorado	Columbus	1836	18,383
Comal	New Braunfels	1846	51,832
Comanche	Comanche	1856	13,381
Concho	Paint Rock	1858	3,044
Cooke	Gainesville	1848	30,777
Coryell	Gatesville	1854	64,213
Cottle	Paducah	1876	2,247
Crane	Crane	1887	4,652
Crockett	Ozona	1875	4,078
Crosby	Crosbytown	1876	7,304
Culberson	Van Horn	1911	3,407
Dallam	Dalhart	1876	5,461
Dallas	Dallas	1846	1,852,810
Dawson	Lamesa	1876	14,349
Deaf Smith	Hereford	1876	19,153
Delta	Cooper	1870	4,857
Denton	Denton	1846	273,525
De Witt	Cuero	1846	18,840
Dickens	Dickens	1876	2,571
Dimmit	Carrizo Springs	1858	10,433
Donley	Clarendon	1876	3,696
Duval	San Diego	1858	12,918
Eastland	Eastland	1858	18,488
Ector	Odessa	1887	118,934
Edwards	Rocksprings	1858	2,266
Ellis	Waxahachie	1849	85,167
El Paso	El Paso	1849	591,610
Erath	Stephenville	1856	27,991
Falls	Marlin	1850	17,712
Fannin	Bonham	1837	24,804
Fayette	La Grange	1837	20,095
Fisher	Roby	1876	4,842
Floyd	Floydada	1876	8,497
Foard	Crowell	1891	1,794
Fort Bend	Richmond	1837	225,421
Franklin	Mount Vernon	1875	7,802

County	County Seat	Year Created	Population
Freestone	Fairfield	1850	15,818
Frio	Pearsall	1871	13,472
Gaines	Seminole	1876	14,123
Galveston	Galveston	1838	217,399
Garza	Post	1876	5,143
Gillespie	Fredericksburg	1848	17,204
Glasscock	Garden City	1887	1,447
Goliad	Goliad	1836	5,980
Gonzales	Gonzales	1836	17,205
Gray	Pampa	1876	23,967
Grayson	Sherman	1846	95,021
Gregg	Longview	1873	104,948
Grimes	Anderson	1846	18,828
Guadalupe	Seguin	1846	64,873
Hale	Plainview	1876	34,671
Hall	Memphis	1876	3,905
Hamilton	Hamilton	1842	7,733
Hansford	Spearman	1876	5,848
Hardeman	Quanah	1858	5,283
Hardin	Kountze	1858	41,320
Harris	Houston	1836	2,818,199
Harrison	Marshall	1839	57,483
Hartley	Channing	1876	3,634
Haskell	Haskell	1858	6,820
Hays	San Marcos	1843	65,614
Hemphill	Canadian	1876	3,720
Henderson	Athens	1846	58,543
Hidalgo	Edinburg	1852	383,545
Hill	Hillsboro	1853	27,146
Hockley	Levelland	1876	24,199
Hood	Granbury	1866	28,981
Hopkins	Sulphur Springs	1846	28,833
Houston	Crockett	1837	21,375
Howard	Big Spring	1876	32,343
Hudspeth	Sierra Blanca	1917	2,915
Hunt	Greenville	1846	64,343
Hutchinson	Stinnett	1876	25,689
Irion	Mertzon	1889	1,629
Jack	Jacksboro	1856	6,981
Jackson	Edna	1835	13,039

County	County Seat	Year Created	Population
Jasper	Jasper	1836	31,102
Jeff Davis	Fort Davis	1887	1,946
Jefferson	Beaumont	1836	239,397
Jim Hogg	Hebbronville	1913	5,109
Jim Wells	Alice	1911	37,679
Johnson	Cleburne	1854	97,165
Jones	Anson	1858	16,490
Karnes	Karnes City	1854	12,455
Kaufman	Kaufman	1848	52,220
Kendall	Boerne	1862	14,589
Kenedy	Sarita	1921	460
Kent	Jayton	1876	1,010
Kerr	Kerrville	1856	36,304
Kimble	Junction	1858	4,122
King	Guthrie	1876	354
Kinney	Brackettville	1850	3,119
Kleberg	Kingsville	1913	30,274
Knox	Benjamin	1858	4,837
Lamar	Paris	1840	43,949
Lamb	Littlefield	1876	15,072
Lampasas	Lampasas	1856	13,521
La Salle	Cotulla	1858	5,254
Lavaca	Hallettsville	1846	18,690
Lee	Giddings	1874	12,854
Leon	Centerville	1846	12,665
Liberty	Liberty	1836	52,726
Limestone	Groesbeck	1846	20,946
Lipscomb	Lipscomb	1876	3,143
Live Oak	George West	1856	9,556
Llano	Llano	1856	11,631
Loving	Mentone	1887	107
Lubbock	Lubbock	1876	222,636
Lynn	Tahoka	1876	6,758
McCulloch	Brady	1856	8,778
McLennan	Waco	1850	189,123
McMullen	Tilden	1858	817
Madison	Madisonville	1853	10,931
Marion	Jefferson	1860	9,984
Martin	Stanton	1876	4,956
Mason	Mason	1858	3,423

County	County Seat	Year Created	Population
Matagorda	Bay City	1836	36,928
Maverick	Eagle Pass	1856	36,378
Medina	Hondo	1848	27,312
Menard	Menard	1858	2,252
Midland	Midland	1885	106,611
Milam	Cameron	1836	22,946
Mills	Goldthwaite	1887	4,531
Mitchell	Colorado City	1876	8,016
Montague	Montague	1857	17,274
Montgomery	Conroe	1837	182,201
Moore	Dumas	1876	17,865
Morris	Daingerfield	1875	13,200
Motley	Matador	1876	1,532
Nacogdoches	Nacogdoches	1836	54,753
Navarro	Corsicana	1846	39,926
Newton	Newton	1846	13,569
Nolan	Sweetwater	1876	16,594
Nueces	Corpus Christi	1846	291,145
Ochiltree	Perryton	1876	9,128
Oldham	Vega	1876	2,278
Orange	Orange	1852	80,509
Palo Pinto	Palo Pinto	1856	25,055
Panola	Carthage	1846	22,035
Parker	Weatherford	1855	64,785
Parmer	Farwell	1876	9,863
Pecos	Fort Stockton	1871	14,675
Polk	Livingston	1846	30,687
Potter	Amarillo	1876	97,874
Presidio	Marfa	1850	6,637
Rains	Emory	1870	6,715
Randall	Canyon	1876	89,673
Reagan	Big Lake	1903	4,514
Real	Leakey	1913	2,412
Red River	Clarksville	1836	14,317
Reeves	Pecos	1883	15,852
Refugio	Refugio	1836	7,976
Roberts	Miami	1876	1,025
Robertson	Franklin	1837	15,511
Rockwall	Rockwall	1873	25,604
Runnels	Ballinger	1858	11,294

County	County Seat	Year Created	Population
Rusk	Henderson	1843	43,735
Sabine	Hemphill	1836	9,586
San Augustine	San Augustine	1836	7,999
San Jacinto	Coldspring	1869	16,372
San Patricio	Sinton	1836	58,749
San Saba	San Saba	1856	5,401
Schleicher	Eldorado	1887	2,990
Scurry	Snyder	1876	18,634
Shackelford	Albany	1858	3,316
Shelby	Center	1836	22,034
Sherman	Stratford	1876	2,858
Smith	Tyler	1846	151,309
Somervell	Glen Rose	1875	5,360
Starr	Rio Grande City	1848	40,518
Stephens	Breckenridge	1858	9,010
Sterling	Sterling City	1891	1,438
Stonewall	Aspermont	1876	2,013
Sutton	Sonora	1887	4,135
Swisher	Tulia	1876	8,133
Tarrant	Fort Worth	1849	1,170,103
Taylor	Abilene	1858	119,655
Terrell	Sanderson	1905	1,410
Terry	Brownfield	1876	13,218
Throckmorton	Throckmorton	1858	1,880
Titus	Mount Pleasant	1846	24,009
Tom Green	San Angelo	1874	98,458
Travis	Austin	1840	576,407
Trinity	Groveton	1850	11,445
Tyler	Woodville	1846	16,646
Upshur	Gilmer	1846	31,370
Upton	Rankin	1887	4,447
Uvalde	Uvalde	1850	23,340
Val Verde	Del Rio	1885	38,721
Van Zandt	Canton	1848	37,944
Victoria	Victoria	1836	74,361
Walker	Huntsville	1846	50,917
Waller	Hempstead	1873	23,390
Ward	Monahans	1887	13,115
Washington	Brenham	1836	26,154
Webb	Laredo	1848	133,239

Chapter 7

County	County Seat	Year Created	Population
Wharton	Wharton	1846	39,955
Wheeler	Wheeler	1876	5,879
Wichita	Wichita Falls	1858	122,378
Wilbarger	Vernon	1858	15,121
Willacy	Raymondville	1911	17,705
Williamson	Georgetown	1848	139,551
Wilson	Floresville	1860	22,650
Winkler	Kermit	1887	8,626
Wise	Decatur	1856	34,679
Wood	Quitman	1850	29,380
Yoakum	Plains	1876	8,786
Young	Graham	1856	18,126
Zapata	Zapata	1858	9,279
Zavala	Crystal City	1858	12,162

* * * * *

Chapter 8 ————————————————

Small Town, Texas

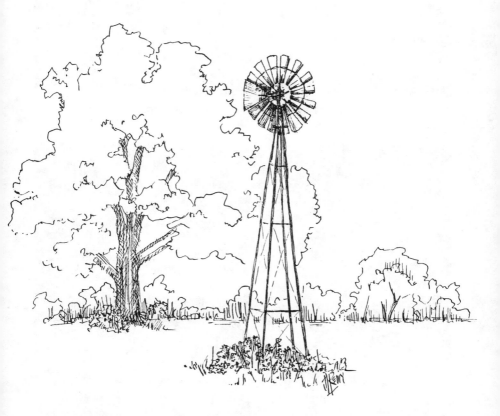

Windmill used to pump water in days past—near Forney, Texas

Texas native field flowers and grasses can be seen throughout Texas on the fence lines and road easements.

The East Texas area is popular with campers, hikers, and nature enthusiasts. This photo was taken on the author's farm in the Alba-Golden area.

Small towns have always fascinated people. What are the people like who prefer the lifestyle of these small towns? The towns around them may be booming but why didn't they grow? Or were these towns the center of activity and then for one reason or another the population slowly dwindled?

The following is a list of towns that have a population of 100 or less. The towns that are listed are either incorporated with a governing body, or are recognized by the postal system and have a post office located in their town, or were listed on the census for 1990:

City Name	County	Population
Ace	Polk	40
Afton	Dickens	100
Aiken	Floyd	60
Alanreed	Gray	60
Albert	Gillespie	25
Altair	Colorado	30
Andice	Williamson	25
Antelope	Jack	65
Arcadia	Shelby	20
Armstrong	Kenedy	20
Art	Mason	18
Artesia Wells	La Salle	30
Austonio	Houston	37
Barnum	Polk	29
Bebe	Gonzales	52
Bee House	Coryell	40
Belmont	Gonzales	60
Ben Franklin	Delta	75
Berclair	Goliad	70
Bergheim	Kendall	22
Best	Reagan	25
Bigfoot	Frio	75
Birome	Hill	31
Black	Parmer	100
Bleiblerville	Austin	71
Bluffton	Llano	75
Booth	Fort Bend	60

City Name	County	Population
Brandon	Hill	80
Briggs	Burnet	92
Brookesmith	Brown	61
Brookston	Lamar	70
Bulverde	Comal	25
Burkett	Coleman	30
Caddo	Stephens	40
Calliham	McMullen	90
Camp Verde	Kerr	41
Carl's Corner	Hill	94
Carlsbad	Tom Green	100
Carlton	Hamilton	70
Carta Valley	Edwards	20
Castell	Llano	72
Cat Spring	Austin	76
Catarina	Dimmit	45
Cayuga	Anderson	56
Cedar Lane	Matagorda	85
Cee Vee	Cottle	71
Centralia	Trinity	26
Chapman Ranch	Nueces	100
Chatfield	Navarro	40
Cheapside	Gonzales	31
Chriesman	Burleson	30
Clay	Burleson	61
Clayton	Panola	79
Clemville	Matagorda	54
Clodine	Fort Bend	31
Collegeport	Matagorda	91
Concan	Uvalde	71
Concepcion	Duval	25
Concord	Leon	28
Corral City	Denton	46
Cost	Gonzales	62
Coy City	Karnes	30
Cypress Mill	Blanco	56
Danevang	Wharton	61

City Name	County	Population
Dawn	Deaf Smith	94
Delmita	Starr	99
Dennis	Parker	86
Dermott	Scurry	5
Doole	McCulloch	74
Doss	Gillespie	75
Dougherty	Floyd	100
Douglass	Nacogdoches	75
Driftwood	Hays	21
Dryden	Terrell	13
Duffau	Erath	76
Dunn	Scurry	75
Egypt	Wharton	26
El Sauz	Starr	85
Elmo	Kaufman	90
Energy	Comanche	65
Etoile	Nacogdoches	70
Fentress	Caldwell	85
Fife	McCulloch	32
Fischer	Comal	20
Flynn	Leon	81
Forest	Cherokee	85
Fort McKavett	Menard	45
Fowlerton	La Salle	100
Francitas	Jackson	30
Fredonia	Mason	50
Freestone	Freestone	35
Geneva	Sabine	100
Girvin	Pecos	30
Glazier	Hemphill	45
Goldsboro	Coleman	30
Goodland	Bailey	25
Gouldbusk	Coleman	70
Greenwood	Wise	76
Guerra	Jim Hogg	75
Guy	Fort Bend	60
Hasse	Comanche	43

City Name	County	Population
Hext	Menard	64
Hochheim	Dewitt	70
Huffman	Harris	50
Impact	Taylor	25
Izoro	Lampasas	31
Jermyn	Jack	75
Jonesville	Harrison	28
Justiceburg	Garza	76
Katemcy	Mason	90
Kellerville	Wheeler	50
Kendalia	Kendall	76
Kent	Culberson	60
Kerrick	Dallam	60
Kildare	Cass	49
Knickerbocker	Tom Green	50
Lake Creek	Delta	60
LaSalle	Jackson	75
Lasara	Willacy	100
Leaday	Coleman	55
Ledbetter	Fayette	76
Lenorah	Martin	70
Leon Junction	Coryell	25
Lingleville	Erath	100
Lipscomb	Lipscomb	45
Lissie	Wharton	70
Lone Grove	Llano	50
Long Mott	Calhoun	76
Lopeno	Zapata	100
Los Ebanos	Hidalgo	100
Los Ybanez	Dawson	83
Lowake	Concho	40
Magnolia Springs	Jasper	80
Maryneal	Nolan	75
Masterson	Moore	15
McCaulley	Fisher	96
McCoy	Atascosa	25
McLeod	Cass	50

City Name	County	Population
McNeil	Travis	70
Mentone	Loving	50
Mereta	Tom Green	75
Mico	Medina	98
Midfield	Matagorda	70
Midkiff	Upton	68
Miller's Cove	Titus	75
Millersview	Concho	75
Millican	Brazos	100
Mineral	Bee	50
Monroe City	Chambers	90
Mound	Coryell	75
Mountain Home	Kerr	96
Muldoon	Fayette	98
Mustang	Navarro	35
Myra	Cooke	70
Nemo	Somervell	56
Newport	Clay-Jack	70
Neylandville	Hunt	94
Normanna	Bee	75
North Zulch	Madison	100
Northfield	Motley	15
Norton	Runnels	76
Oakland	Colorado	80
Opdyke West	Hockley	100
Ottine	Gonzales	90
Otto	Falls	85
Paluxy	Hood	76
Panna Maria	Karnes	96
Pear Valley	McCulloch	37
Peaster	Parker	80
Peggy	Atascosa	20
Pendleton	Bell	60
Pennington	Trinity-Houston	100
Penwell	Ector	74
Pep	Hockley	50
Perry	Falls	96

Chapter 8

City Name	County	Population
Pettit	Hockley	26
Petty	Lamar	100
Pickton	Hopkins	90
Pierce	Wharton	49
Pipe Creek	Bandera	66
Plum	Fayette	95
Prairie Lea	Caldwell	100
Purmela	Coryell	61
Quail	Collingsworth	92
Quintana	Brazoria	51
Rainbow	Somervell	76
Randolph	Fannin	70
Red Rock	Bastrop	100
Red Springs	Baylor	81
Ringgold	Montague	100
Rio Frio	Real	50
Riomedina	Medina	53
Rockwood	Coleman	80
Rocky Mound	Camp	53
Roganville	Jasper	100
Romayor	Liberty	96
Roosevelt	Kimble	98
Round Mountain	Blanco	59
Round Top	Fayette	81
Rye	Liberty	76
Salt Flat	Hudspeth	35
Sandy	Blanco	25
Santa Elena	Starr	64
Sargent	Matagorda	76
Segno	Polk	80
Shafter	Presidio	31
Silver	Coke	60
Singleton	Grimes	44
Sisterdale	Kendall	63
South Bend	Young	100
South Plains	Floyd	25
Speaks	Lavaca	60

City Name	County	Population
Spofford	Kinney	68
Staples	Guadalupe	75
Star	Mills	85
Sublime	Lavaca	75
Summerfield	Castro	60
Sumner	Lamar	80
Sun Valley	Lamar	60
Sylvester	Fisher	79
Tarpley	Bandera	30
Tarzan	Martin	80
Telegraph	Kimble	3
Telico	Ellis	95
Tell	Childress	63
Tennyson	Coke	35
Terlingua	Brewster	25
Texon	Reagon	35
The Grove	Coryell	65
Thomaston	De Witt	45
Todd Mission	Grimes	54
Tokio	Terry	60
Toyahvale	Reeves	60
Tuleta	Bee	98
Turnertown	Rusk	76
Twitty	Wheeler	60
Valera	Coleman	80
Valley Spring	Llano	50
Vanderpool	Bandera	20
Verhalen	Reeves	52
Veribest	Tom Green	40
Vigo Park	Swisher	31
Voca	McCulloch	56
Voss	Coleman	20
Warda	Fayette	67
Waring	Kendall	73
Warrenton	Fayette	50
Wayside	Armstrong	40
Wellborn	Brazos	100

City Name	County	Population
Whitt	Parker	38
Whon	Coleman	15
Willow City	Gillespie	75
Winchester	Fayette	50
Wrightsboro	Gonzales	76

Thank You . . .

When I first started writing this book, over 300 Chambers and individuals responded to my requests. I am sorry that I could not use all the information that was sent to me.

The following is a list of people and organizations who sent me information found in this book. I hope I have not left anyone out. I truly wish to thank everyone who helped me in my research!

Chamber of Commerce - Abilene
Miss Cleo Congrady - Alvin Museum Society - Alvin
Convention & Visitors Bureau - Amarillo
Chamber of Commerce - Anahauc
Joy Fowler - Chamber of Commerce - Andrews County
Chamber of Commerce - Anson
Chamber of Commerce - Aransas Pass
Convention & Visitors Bureau - Arlington
Chamber of Commerce - Athens
Chamber of Commerce - Atlanta Area
Chamber of Commerce - Austin
Texas Parks and Wildlife Dept. - Austin
Kerri Crawford - Chamber of Commerce - Azle
Karen Riddle - Chamber of Commerce - Baird
Bobbie Shelton - Chamber of Commerce - Ballinger
Patricia Moore - Convention and Visitors Bureau - Bandera
    County
Chamber of Commerce - Bastrop
Convention & Visitors Bureau - Beaumont
Chamber of Commerce - Bee County
Chamber of Commerce - Bellmead
Lorie Krueger - Chamber of Commerce - Belton Area
Mamie Lee Dodds - Chamber of Commerce - Big Spring Area
Betty Paschal - Chamber of Commerce - Bishop

Thank You . . .

Chamber of Commerce - Bolivar Peninsula
Chamber of Commerce - Bonham
Chamber of Commerce - Borger
Chamber of Commerce - Bowie
Nancy Ford - Chamber of Commerce - Brownfield
Chamber of Commerce - Brady
Chamber of Commerce - Bridge City
D.C. Sipes, D.C. - State Historical Commission - Bridgeport
Chamber of Commerce - Brownwood
Pam Hanning - Chamber of Commerce - Buffalo
Mindy L. Simmons - Chamber of Commerce - Burkburnett
Chamber of Commerce - Burnet
Fort Croghan Museum - Burnet
Dee Orlopp - Chamber of Commerce - Caldwell
Chamber of Commerce - Calvert
Edward Aycock - Chamber of Commerce - Cameron Area
Joe Collins - Chamber of Commerce - Canton
Chamber of Commerce - Castroville
Historical Society - Cedar Hill
Chamber of Commerce - Centerville Area
W.T. Nelson - Chamber of Commerce - Childress
Chamber of Commerce - Cisco
Claudette Alderman - Chamber of Commerce - Clear Lake Area
Perry D. Gott - Chamber of Commerce - Cleburne
Chamber of Commerce - Clifton
"Lil" Stallman - Chamber of Commerce - Columbus Area
Darlene Causey - Chamber of Commerce - Comanche
Faye McDaniel - Chamber of Commerce - Comfort
James H. Conrad, Ph.D. - East Texas State University -
    Commerce
Chamber of Commerce - Conroe
Karen Wheat - Delta County Public Library - Cooper
Chamber of Commerce - Copperas Cove
Convention & Visitors Bureau - Corpus Christi Area
Chamber of Commerce - Cotulla-LaSalle
Chamber of Commerce - Crane County
Deborah Seibert - Chamber of Commerce - Crosby/Huffman
Chamber of Commerce - Cuero

Convention & Visitors Bureau - Dallas
Kim Dillon - Chamber of Commerce - Del Rio
Anna H. McKinney - Chamber of Commerce - Denison Area
Charlotte Kemp - Chamber of Commerce - Denton
Chamber of Commerce - Denver City
Patsy Jones - Chamber of Commerce - Dublin
Chamber of Commerce - Dumas
William H. Harrison - Eagle Lake
Chamber of Commerce - Eagle Lake
Dana Curtis - Chamber of Commerce - Early
Chamber of Commerce - Eastland
Chamber of Commerce - Edinburg
Hidalgo County Historical Museum - Edinburg
Convention & Visitors Bureau - El Paso
Chamber of Commerce - Elgin
Chamber of Commerce - Emory
Chamber of Commerce - Ennis Area
Chamber of Commerce - Falfurrias
Chamber of Commerce - Floresville
Tammy Leeson - Chamber of Commerce - Floydada
Chamber of Commerce - Forney
Chamber of Commerce - Fort Bend
Nessye Mae Roach - Fort Davis
Convention & Visitors Bureau - Fort Worth
Penny C. Reeh - Chamber of Commerce - Fredericksburg
Chamber of Commerce - Ft. Stockton
Cindy Nichols - Chamber of Commerce - Gainesville
Convention and Visitors Bureau - Galveston Island
Chamber of Commerce - Gatesville
Mary Loescher - Convention and Visitors Bureau - Georgetown
Chamber of Commerce - Giddings
Upshur County Historical Commission - Gilmer
Joyce Morrison - Upshur County Library - Gilmer
Dee Colvin - Chamber of Commerce - Gladewater
Chamber of Commerce and Agriculture - Golzales
Louise Witkowski - Young County Historical Commission - Graham
Chamber of Commerce - Graham

Thank You . . .

Convention and Visitors Bureau - Granbury
Convention and Visitors Bureau - Grapevine
Nancy Merchant - Chamber of Commerce - Greater Boerne
    Area
Joan Meadows - Chamber of Commerce - Greater Cleveland
Cindy Langley Morales - Chamber of Commerce - Greater
    Devine
Chamber of Commerce - Greenville
Historical Commission - Gregg County
Kathy Biehn - Chamber of Commerce - Grimes County
Lee Rogers - Chamber of Commerce - Groves
David Allex - Chamber of Commerce - Harlingen
Chamber of Commerce - Hempstead
Carolyn Jones - Deaf Smith Chamber of Commerce - Hereford
Chamber of Commerce - Hitchcock
Chamber of Commerce - Hondo
Mary Anne Thurman - Chamber of Commerce - Honey Grove
Chamber of Commerce - Hopkins County
Robert Nowak - Convention and Visitors Bureau - Houston
Polly Mays - Historical Society - Howard County
Chamber of Commerce - Hughes Springs
Chamber of Commerce - Huntsville - Walker
Chamber of Commerce - Ingleside
Chamber of Commerce - Iraan
Chamber of Commerce - Italy
Darlene Maxwell - Chamber of Commerce - Jacksboro
Tammy Harvey - Chamber of Commerce & Agriculture -
    Jackson County
Chamber of Commerce - Jewett
Chamber of Commerce - Karnes City
Chamber of Commerce - Katy
Chamber of Commerce - Kaufman
Chamber of Commerce - Kermit
Texas Hill Co. Tourism Assoc. - Kerrville
Kerr County Historical Commission - Kerrville
Chamber of Commerce - Kerville
Chamber of Commerce - Kilgore
Convention and Visitors Bureau - Killeen

Chamber of Commerce - Kingsville
Barbara Boss - Convention and Visitors Bureau - Kleberg
    County
Chamber of Commerce - Lake Buchanan/Inks Lake
Chamber of Commerce - Lake Corpus Christi
Chamber of Commerce - Lake Whitney
Chamber of Commerce - Laredo
Mary Anne - Chamber of Commerce - Liberty-Dayton
Jackie Hatfield - Chamber of Commerce - Llano County
Chamber of Commerce - Lockhart
Howard W. Rosser - East Texas Tourism Association - Longview
Convention and Visitors Bureau - Longview
Adam J. Saunders - Visitors and Convention Bureau - Lufkin
Susan Ward - Chamber of Commerce - Luling
Shirley Karznia - Chamber of Commerce - Mansfield
Chamber of Commerce - Marathon
Chamber of Commerce - Marshall
Chamber of Commerce - Martin County
Gloria Nebgen - Chamber of Commerce - Mason County
Chamber of Commerce - Mathis
Chamber of Commerce - McAllen
Mendy J. Stovall - Chamber of Commerce - McKinney
Delores McWhorter - Chamber of Commerce - Memphis
Chamber of Commerce - Merkel
Jane Bright - Roberts County Museum - Miami
Cheryl Daniel - Chamber of Commerce - Midland
Chamber of Commerce - Mineola
Chamber of Commerce - Mineral Wells
Gabriela Alvarez - Chamber of Commerce - Mission
Lisa Casados - Chamber of Commerce - Moore County &
    Dumas
Ruby Goodman - Chamber of Commerce - Morton
Marie Muse - Chamber of Commerce - Mount Pleasant
Ava Harmon - Convention and Visitors Bureau - Nacogdoches
Chamber of Commerce - New Boston
Chamber of Commerce - New Braunfels
Chamber of Commerce - Nocona
L.J. Dean - Chamber of Commerce - Nueces Canyon

Thank You . . .

Pat Owsley - Chamber of Commerce - Odessa
West Texas Travel Council - Odessa
Cynthia Jackson - Chamber of Commerce - Orange
Chamber of Commerce - Overton
Convention and Visitors Bureau - Palestine
Chamber of Commerce - Panola County
Chamber of Commerce - Pasadena
Ruth A. Higdon - Pearsall
Sheiladawn Rowinsky-Caddell - Chamber of Commerce -
    Pearsall
Chamber of Commerce - Perryton-Ochiltree
Liza E. Gonzalez - Chamber of Commerce - Pharr
Antiques Center - Pittsburg
Ramona Robert - Plainview
Chamber of Commerce - Plainview
Sharon Bartles - City of Plano
Alice Parker - Chamber of Commerce - Pleasanton
Longhorn Museum - Pleasanton
Chamber of Commerce - Port Isabel
Jerry Stanley - Chamber of Commerce and Agriculture - Port
    Lavaca-Calhoun
Dru Ann Laws - Chamber of Commerce - Post
Bertha Woods - Chamber of Commerce - Quanah
Chamber of Commerce - Quitman
Carol Stewart - Chamber of Commerce - Rockdale
Chamber of Commerce - Rockport-Fulton
Chamber of Commerce and Agriculture - Rosebud
Chamber of Commerce - Rosenberg-Richmond
Dave Nagel - Mayor - Round Top
Mary Alice Ethridge - Chamber of Commerce - Rowlett
Chamber of Commerce - Rusk
Beth Morrison - Chamber of Commerce - Saginaw
Chamber of Commerce - Saint Jo
Sue Yetter - Stonewall Saloon Museum - Saint Jo
Chamber of Commerce - San Angelo
Daughters of the Republic of Texas - San Antonio
Convention and Visitors Bureau - San Antonio
Liz - Chamber of Commerce - San Augustine

Pat - Public Library - San Augustine
Liz Ware - Chamber of Commerce - San Augustine County
Frances Stovall - Hays County Historical Commission - San
    Marcos
Chamber of Commerce - San Saba County
May Belle Vecera - Chamber of Commerce - Sealy
B.J. Comingore - Seguin
Chamber of Commerce - Seminole
Treva McNeill - Chamber of Commerce - Seymour
Laticia Bomar - Chamber of Commerce - Shelby County
Norma Goetz - Chamber of Commerce - Shiner
Peggy Row - Chamber of Commerce - Smithville
Chamber of Commerce - Snyder
Jo-Ann E. Palmer - Sutton County Historical Society - Sonora
Chamber of Commerce - Sonora
Convention and Visitors Bureau - South Padre Island
Donald L. Cobb - Chamber of Commerce - Stamford
Chamber of Commerce - Starr County
Chamber of Commerce - Stonewall
J.R. Lasley - Chamber of Commerce - Stratford
Donna Bailey - Chamber of Commerce - Sweeny
Ruth Mantor - Taylor
Mary Irving - Railroad and Pioneer Museum - Temple
City of Temple - Temple
Terrell State Hospital - Terrell
Chamber of Commerce - Terrell
Chamber of Commerce - Texarkana
Cathy Wood - Chamber of Commerce - The Colony
Chamber of Commerce - Tyler
Jeanne Buck - Chamber of Commerce - Tyler County
Chamber of Commerce - Upshur County
Lana Tolleson - Convention and Visitors Bureau - Uvalde
Russell Kuykendall - Convention and Visitors Bureau - Van
    Horn
Mary Jane Rudolph - Chamber of Commerce - Vernon
Chamber of Commerce - Victoria
Tourist Information Center - Waco
Chamber of Commerce - Washington County

Thank You . . .

Chamber of Commerce - Waxahachie
Jean Bryan - Chamber of Commerce - Weatherford
Chamber of Commerce - Weimar
Dorothy Warren - Chamber of Commerce - West
Chamber of Commerce - West Columbia
West Columbia Historical Museum - West Columbia
Marilyn S. Hunt - Chamber of Commerce & Agriculture -
    Wharton
Convention and Visitors Bureau - Wichita Falls
Chamber of Commerce - Wills Point
Lori Witten - Chamber of Commerce - Wimberley
A. Emerson - Chamber of Commerce - Yoakum
Chamber of Commerce - Zapata County

Other References

Texas State Travel Guide - published by the Texas Department of Transportation, Austin, Texas

Texas Almanac - 1992-93 - published by the *Dallas Morning News*, Dallas, Texas

Texas Travel Handbook - published by the Texas Department of Highways & Public Transportation, Austin, Texas

Index

4-H Club, 38, 111

A

Abilene, 31, 46, 60
Abilene, Chili Super Bowl, 91
Abilene, West Texas Fair, 89
Abilene, Wind Festival, 91
Abilene State Park, 60
Agreda, Mother Maria de, 2-3
Ais Indians, 78
Alabama-Coushatta Indian
    Reservation, 114
Alamo, cornerstone, 47, 53, 147
Alamo battle survivors, 48
Alamo bell, 85
Alamo Village, 138
Albany, 47
Alibates Flint Quarries National
    Monument, 39
Alice, 55
Alligator Head, 76
Alto, 36, 49
Alvin, 60
Amarillo, 30, 33, 106, 107
Anahuac, 9, 72, 92, 111
Andrews, 60
Andrews County, 60, 136
Andrews Prairie Dog Town Camper
    Park, 84
Andrews, Richard, 48
Angelina County, 17
Angelo State University, 41
Angleton, 4
Anson, 67
Anthony, 56
Aransas County, 126
Aransas National Wildlife Refuge,
    119, 120, 123
Aransas Pass, 4, 89, 91
Arbor Day, 22
Archive War, 47
Arlington, 32, 137
Arlington, Sewing Machine Museum,
    86
Arlington, Virginia, 28

Ashbel Smith Building, 36
Astrodome, 38
Athens, 5, 55, 107, 91-92
Atlanta, 30, 55, 85, 90, 91
Aunt Jemimah, 62
Austin's colony, 23
Austin, 28, 30, 46, 47, 50, 87, 92,
    118, 119, 120, 131, 133
Austin, L.B.J. Library and Museum,
    87
Austin, Stephen F., 59, 81, 131, 138
Ayers, Claude, 9
Azle, 31, 136

B

B.S. Steinhagen Lake, 82
Bailey, James Britton, 4
Bailey, Robert, 24
Baird, 5, 61
Ballinger, 61, 137
Balmorhea State Park, 30
Balmorhea, 19-20
Bandera County, 62, 108, 122, 137
Bandera, 55, 62, 94, 107, 122, 137
Barnes, Howard, 41
Barrow, Bonnie, 10
Barrow, Clyde, 10
Bass, Sam, 75
Bastrop, 57, 61, 122, 137
Bastrop Advertiser, 30
Battle of Concepcion, 48
Battle of Gonzales, 131
Battle of Nacogdoches, 48
Battle of San Jacinto, 147
Battle of Velasco, 132
Baylor University, 43, 140
Bean, Judge Roy, 12, 138
Beason's, 33
Beaumont, 55, 61, 88, 92
Beaumont Police Museum, 86
Becton, Dr. E.P., 11
Bee County, 61
Belle Starr, 8
Belton, 31, 34, 89
Bend, 123

Menard, 25
Mercedes, 18, 143
Meridian, 57
Merkel, 72
Mesquite, 56, 90
Mesquiteville, 71
Mexia, 121, 134
Miami, 18, 73, 100
Midland, 122
Midland, 38-39, 58, 85, 88
Miguel Aleman Suspension Bridge, 42
Milam County, 54
Millsap, 128
Mineola, 18, 51, 73
Mineral Wells, 39
Mission Ampuero, 78
Mission Concepcion, 42
Mission Espiritu Santo, 34, 113-114
Mission Tejas State Historic Park, 59
Mission, 77
Missouri, Kansas & Texas Railroad, 51
Mobil Oil, 36
Monahans Sandhills State Park, 104
Money Hill, 4
Montague County, 6, 61
Montell, 63
Montezuma, 54
Montgomery County, 64
Moody, 58
Moody, Governor Dan, 80
Moore County, 139
Morgan, 54
Morton Cemetery, 41
Morton Salt mine, 28
Mother Maria de Agreda, 2-3
Mount Pleasant, 73
Mountain Home, 134
Mudville, 79
Muleshoe, 90, 119
Munday, 108
Munson, Thomas V., 68
Mustang Island, 53
Mustang Island State Park, 119
Mustangs of Las Colinas, 35
Myers, Col. John Jacob, 16-17

N

Nachitoches, 19
Nacodgoches, 19, 29, 39, 100, 145
Naples, 74

National Fish Hatchery, 127
National Scientific Balloon Facility, 75
Natural Food Associates, 84-85
Naval Station Ingleside, 71
Navasota, 39
Neches River, 32, 62
Nederland, 68
New Birmingham Trail, 25
New Boston, 74
New Braunfels, 39, 86, 122, 124
New London, 19
New York, Texas, 60
Newton, 119
Nickel Baptist Church, 40
Nickleville, 82
Nimitz, Admiral, 69
Nip and Tuck, 53
Nocona, 89
Nocona Boot Co., 89
Nocona, Chief Peta, 21
Norse community, 90
Nueces River, 73

O

O'Donnell, 46
O-Bar, 31
O. Henry, 50
O.S. Ranch, 21
Oak Grove Cemetery, 39
Ochiltree County, 40
Odessa Rodeo, 39-40
Odessa, 29, 74, 100, 111, 145
Ogletree Gap Valley, 67
Old Boston, 73-74
Old San Antonio Road, 19
Olney, 119
Orange, 74
Ozona, 51, 81, 148

P

P.O.W. camp, 7, 30, 48, 57
Pace, Admiral Ernest, 62
Padre Island, 148
Paducah, 51
Palestine, 32, 40, 97, 100, 118
Palmetto State Park, 123
Palmito Hill Battlefield, 49
Palo Duro Canyon, 91, 106, 122
Panna Maria, 29, 58
Panola, 63

Index

San Antonio, 30, 42, 47, 58, 89,
 101-102, 124, 126, 127
San Augustine, 41, 58, 78
San Felipe, 62
San Felipe de Austin, 59
San Francisco de los Tejas, 58
San Jacinto, 144
San Jacinto Battleground State
 Historical Park, 47
San Jacinto Monument, 133
San Marcos River, 125, 133
San Marcos, 50, 78
San Saba, 112-113
San Saba County, 147
Santa Ana National Wildlife Refuge,
 124
Santa Anna Mountain, 64
Sattler, 50
Scurry County, 78
Sealy, 147
Seguin, 30, 78, 86, 104, 147
Seminole Canyon State Park, 85
Seymour, Fish Day, 102
Shamrock, 46
Shelby County, 9, 33, 62
Shelby County courthouse, 28
Sheppard Air Force Base, 43
Shiner, 42, 66, 148
Shirley, Myra Bell, 8
Shivers, Governor Allan, 104
Shoal Point, 57
Sierra Blanca, 135
Singer Sewing Machine, 4
Singer, John, 4
Sinton, 121
Six Shooter Junction, 68, 75
Slaughter, George Webb, 60
small towns of Texas, 159-166
Smith-Hoyt-Youngs House, 30
Smithville, 127, 148
Snyder, 78, 102
Snyder County, 78
Sodom, 18
Somerset, 40
Sonora, 3, 103, 107, 113
Southfork Ranch, 146
Rowlett, 146
Southwest Texas State University, 50
Southwestern Christian College, 42-43
Southwestern University, 37
Spindletop, 55, 61, 137

Splendora, 64
Spoetzl Brewery, 42
Spring, 51
St. Clare Monastery Miniature Horse
 Farm, 88
St. Denis, 17
St. John, John, 25
St. Louis Society Building, 10
St. Mary's Cathedral, 59
Stafford Municipal School District, 28
Staggers Point, 15
Stamford, Texas Cowboy Reunion,
 102
Stanton, 52, 79
Starr, Belle, 8
State Capitol Building, 27, 28, 30, 143
State flags, 130
State Meat Inspection Training
 School, 43
Steward, Dr. Azle, 31
Stewart, Charles W., 39
Stonewall, 52
Strait, George, 75
Stratford, 78, 113
strawberry, 29, 58
Strecker Museum, 43
Sugar Land, 79, 88
Sulphur Springs, 11, 79, 85
Sundance Kid, 12
Sunrise Wind, 22
Sweeny, 4
Sweeny, John, 4
Sweetwater, 95, 107

T

Tanglefoot, 79
Taylor, 56, 80
Taylor, Claudia Alta, 49, 60
Taylor County, 10
Taylorsville, 54, 56
Temple, 22, 79, 80, 103, 140
Terlingua, 69
Terrell, 12-13
Terrell, R.A., 42
Terrell State Hospital, 42
Texarkana, 80, 139, 148
Texas & Pacific Railway, 18
Texas A&M University, 46, 81, 86,
 108, 132
Texas champion water oak, 33
Texas City, 57, 121

Index